HEAVEN CRAWLEY
FRANCK DÜVELL
KATHARINE JONES
SIMON MCMAHON
NANDO SIGONA

UNRAVELLING EUROPE'S 'MIGRATION CRISIS'

Journeys over land and sea

POLICY PRESS SHORTS INSIGHTS

First published in Great Britain in 2018 by

Policy Press
University of Bristol
1-9 Old Park Hill
Bristol
BS2 8BB
UK
t: +44 (0)117 954 5940
pp-info@bristol.ac.uk
www.policypress.co.uk

North America office:
Policy Press
c/o The University of Chicago Press
1427 East 60th Street
Chicago, IL 60637, USA
t: +1 773 702 7700
f: +1 773 702 9756
sales@press.uchicago.edu
www.press.uchicago.edu

British Library Cataloguing in Publication Data
A catalogue record for this book is available from the British Library.

Library of Congress Cataloging-in-Publication Data
A catalog record for this book has been requested.

ISBN 978-1-4473-4321-9 (paperback)
ISBN 978-1-4473-4323-3 (ePub)
ISBN 978-1-4473-4324-0 (Mobi)
ISBN 978-1-4473-4322-6 (ePDF)

Cover design by Policy Press
Front cover: image kindly supplied by Heaven Crawley

Contents

List of figures

List of boxes

Acronyms

CSOs	Civil Society Organisations
EC	European Commission
EU	European Union
FRONTEX	European Border and Coast Guard Agency
FYROM	Former Yugoslav Republic of Macedonia
FSA	Free Syrian Army
HRW	Human Rights Watch
IOM	International Organisation for Migration
IS	Islamic State
MOAS	Migrant Offshore Aid Station
MSF	Médecins Sans Frontières
OHCHR	Office of the High Commission(er) for Human Rights
SAR	Search and Rescue
UN	United Nations
UNDP	United Nations Development Programme
UNHCR	United Nations High Commission(er) for Refugees
UNODC	United Nations Office on Drugs and Crime

Notes on the authors

Heaven Crawley is Professor of International Migration at Coventry University's Centre for Trust, Peace and Social Relations (CTPSR), Senior Research Associate at the Overseas Development Institute (ODI) and Senior Research Fellow at the Refugee Law Initiative. Heaven's research focuses on the lived experiences of refugees and migrants. Over the past 25 years she has worked in a range of institutional settings including government, civil society and the UN, and published extensively on asylum and migration policy and practice in the UK and Europe.

Franck Düvell is Associate Professor and Senior Researcher at the Centre on Migration, Policy and Society (COMPAS) at the University of Oxford, a Senior member of the Common Room of St Antony's College, Oxford, member of South East European Studies at Oxford and advisor of the Migration Research Centre at Koc University, Istanbul. He has researched European and international migration for over 20 years, published nine books and over 40 journal articles. He has also advised a wide range of stakeholders.

Katharine Jones is a Senior Research Fellow at Coventry University's Centre for Trust, Peace and Social Relations. Educated at the Universities of Newcastle upon Tyne and Manchester, Katharine has more than 16 years' experience of conducting migration-related research in a wide range of institutional settings. Her work focuses on the human rights impacts and business models of the migration industry. She regularly advises international organisations and international NGOs on this topic.

Simon McMahon joined Coventry University's Centre for Trust, Peace and Social Relations as a Research Fellow in September 2014. He has a PhD from King's College London and has been a visiting researcher at the European University Institute in Italy, the Pompeu Fabra University in Spain and the Colegio de la Frontera Sur in Mexico. Simon has published several books and journal articles and has also written for outlets such as the *Guardian* and *The Conversation*.

Nando Sigona is Deputy Director of the University of Birmingham's Institute for Research into Superdiversity. His research interests include: undocumented migration, statelessness, child and youth migration, Roma politics and forced displacement. His work has been published in a range of international academic journals and books. He is a founding editor of the journal *Migration Studies* and lead editor of *Global Migration and Social Change* book series at Policy Press. He has written for *Newsweek*, the *Independent*, *Libération*, *OpenDemocracy* and *The Conversation*.

Acknowledgements

Between September 2015 and November 2016, a team of researchers led by the Centre for Trust, Peace and Social Relations (CTPSR) at Coventry University, working in collaboration with the University of Birmingham's Institute for Research into Superdiversity and the Centre on Migration, Policy and Society at the University of Oxford, conducted research into the 'migration crisis' at the borders of Southern Europe.

We would like to thank our international partners from Greece (ELIAMEP), Italy (FIERI), Turkey (Yasar University) and Malta (People for Change Foundation (PfC)) for their contribution to the research, specifically Dia Anagnostou (ELIAMEP), Ferruccio Pastore (FIERI), Ayselin Yildiz (Yasar), Jean-Pierre Gauci (PfC), Christine Cassar (PfC) and Ismini Karydopoulou (GFR). Particular thanks are due to those who assisted with data collection in the case study countries including Ioannis Chapsos, Chiara Denaro, Giulia Gonzales, Fiona McKinnon, Gokay Ozerim, Anastassia Papakonstantinou, Abdul Fatah Rabiei, Ester Salis, Dimitris Skleparis and Lucia Slot. Aurelie Broeckerhoff, Dan Range and Esra Kaytaz (CTPSR) made an important contribution to data entry and analysis. Simon McMahon (CTPSR) built the database on which this report is based. Chris Davies (WSP | Parsons Brinckerhoff) kindly assisted with the production of the map. Victoria Pittman, Shannon Kneis, Kathryn King and Ruth Wallace at Policy Press made the process of producing this book quick and straightforward. Thank you all.

Our research has benefited immensely from the insights, experience and expertise of the large number of people with whom we have worked and discussed our ideas and findings over the past year. We are grateful in particular for the contribution of Michael Collyer (University of Sussex), Jeff Crisp (Oxford University) and Albert Kraler (ICMPD) as well as the members of our Advisory Group at different stages in the research process: Simona Ardovino, Miriam Edding (WatchtheMed), Aurelie Ponthieu (MSF), George Joseph (Caritas Sweden), Michele Levoy (PICUM), Aspasia Papadopoulou (ECRE), Elisa de Pieri (Amnesty International) and Roger Zetter (Refugee Studies Centre, Oxford University). We would also like to thank the participants of the roundtable held in Oxford (March 2016), the policy workshops held in Rome (May 2016) and Athens (June 2016), IASFM conference in Poznan (July 2016), IMISCOE annual conference (July 2016), side-event at the UN Summit for Refugees and Migrants in New York (September 2016), launch event in Brussels (November 2016), IMISCOE spring conference (February 2017) and meetings with the European Commission's Joint Research Centre (JRC) in Ispra and Brussels (February and June 2017), for their contribution to our thinking. Any errors are, of course, our own.

Finally, and most importantly, we would like to thank all of those who contributed directly to this research and, in particular, the hundreds of refugees and migrants who crossed the Mediterranean in 2015 and were willing to share their stories with us. We hope that this book contributes to a deeper understanding of their experiences.

This work was supported by the Economic and Social Research Council [grant number ES/N013506/01]. Further information about the research including all of our publications and events can be found on our project website www.medmig.info.

Policy and law correct at the time of writing, July 2017.

Foreword

Although Europe's so-called 'migration crisis' is often presented as something new, the movement of people across the Mediterranean to Europe is not. MSF has been providing assistance to people crossing the Mediterranean to Europe since the autumn of 2002, when an MSF team started working in Lampedusa reception centre, providing new arrivals with medical care. Since then we have been assisting people in Greece and Italy and at multiple points along the route.

The work of MSF includes providing first assistance, medical and psychological support, shelter, water, sanitation and essential relief items at reception centres and transit camps, as well as providing food and clothing. But it also, inevitably, involves listening to the stories of those we meet, hearing about the reasons why they left their homes and families, what happened to them on their journey, why they felt that had no choice other than to move on and how they sustained the physical and psychological injuries we try to heal.

The year 2015 was a particularly difficult one. MSF was challenged to respond to an unparalleled flow of people seeking protection in Europe. We were at the receiving end of a policy-made crisis. We set up mobile clinics and shelters at the European borders, in Greece, Italy, Serbia and Croatia. In the absence of safe and legal routes available to those fleeing violence, human rights violations and wars, we launched search and rescue operations to save the lives of those forced to take to the sea.

The stories were heard resonate strongly with those reported in this book. Most did not choose to leave their countries of origin, rather they fled bombing, detention, torture and destitution. For many, the migration journey over land and sea was the main cause of illness and suffering regardless of the trajectory they had been forced to take. This book provides a deep understanding of the complexity of these trajectories, bearing witness to the violence and neglect that runs through the experiences of those on the move.

In so doing, this book exposes the misguided and politically motivated assumptions that dominated Europe's response in 2015 and 2016. These assumptions continue to shape the direction of policy even today. Misconceptions, arbitrary categorisation and the politically convenient labelling of the people reaching Europe frame, often in a skewed way, the focus and direction of that response. Generic legal terminologies cannot fully reflect the complexity of people's migratory movements, their deep trauma and their need for protection and assistance. The failure to listen to the stories of those on the move, to recognise their overwhelming urge to seek safety, or even acknowledge their humanity has undermined both the legal framework for protection and assistance and our sense of who we are and what we believe in. Taking notice of the findings of the MEDMIG research and listening to the stories in this book would be an important first step in putting that right.

Dr Joanne Liu,
International President of Médecins sans Frontières (MSF)

ONE

The view from Europe

Box 1.1: The story of Michael and Niyat from Eritrea[1]

When Michael and his wife Niyat left Eritrea in September 2015 they had little idea of what lay ahead of them. Like many Eritreans, Michael had been conscripted into the army at a young age. After 14 years of being forced to work for virtually nothing, and with no release date in sight, he decided he could take no more. Taking advantage of a period of leave, Michael and Niyat left Eritrea, crossing the Red Sea by boat to Sudan with the help of fishermen whom they met on the shore. When they arrived in Port Sudan they made their way to Khartoum by bus but after living there for one year they moved on because they no longer felt safe. To escape, Michael and Niyat paid smugglers to take them to Libya across the Sahara Desert. It was a very challenging journey. Both were beaten by the smugglers. They were also held captive by the smugglers and forced to call family and friends to raise money for additional payments demanded for the journey across the sea. When they had been at sea for around five hours they were rescued by an Italian ship. Realising that Niyat was heavily pregnant, Italian officials arranged for the couple to be taken to a hospital in Malta (which was closer than Italy) where their daughter was born the following day. Michael and Niyat told us that they had never intended to come to Europe, and certainly not to Malta, but as their journey unfolded they believed they had no alternative. They had only sought to find safety and a place where they could make a life for themselves and their new baby.

Michael and Niyat are just two of an estimated 1,011,712 refugees and migrants[2] who crossed the Mediterranean to Europe in search of safety and a better life during 2015. At least 3,770 women, men and children are thought to have died trying to make this journey (IOM, 2016a). European political debate and media coverage during 2015 focused on the drama of perilous journeys across the Mediterranean Sea, the smugglers, the hardships endured by refugees and migrants during the journey and on arrival in Europe, and the political, economic, social and cultural implications of increased migration for European Union (EU) Member States. This 'story' of migration continued into 2016 and 2017. Events were widely perceived as constituting a 'crisis': of uncontrolled and unregulated movement into Europe, of the political failure of states to respond collectively, and of the international community's failure to address the pressing humanitarian needs of those arriving on Europe's shores.

Migration across the Mediterranean in 2015

How Europe's 'migration crisis' was presented reflects and reinforces a particular way of thinking about the dynamics of migration. Politicians and policymakers across Europe have largely talked about the arrival of refugees and migrants in 2015 as an *unprecedented* event, a single coherent flow of people that came 'from nowhere', suddenly and unexpectedly pressing against the continent's southern border. Media coverage gave the impression of a linear, uninterrupted flow of people heading towards Europe, most commonly represented by straight arrows on a map linking two distinct areas (see also Mainwaring and Brigden, 2016). This was very much a view from Europe.

As a result, there was very little interest in the 'back stories' of those arriving; instead, policymakers generalised and made often erroneous assumptions about what happened between someone leaving their home country and arriving on the shores of Europe. This has led to, at best, a partial account of the reasons why people were prepared to risk everything by boarding mostly flimsy, unseaworthy, overloaded vessels in order to make the dangerous journey across the Mediterranean. The focus on the *scale* of migration and the drama of maritime rescues and arrival came at the expense of a more nuanced understanding of the, sometimes vast, differences in the usually fragmented and protracted journeys of refugees and migrants.

Drawing on the experiences and voices of the women and men who arrived in Europe during 2015, this book tells the largely untold story of Europe's 'migration crisis'. The experiences of people like Michael and Niyat, a young Eritrean couple seeking the opportunities that many of us take for granted, provide new insights into the dynamics of migration to Europe. Privileging the perspective of refugees and migrants themselves, this book provides an in-depth analysis of the experiences of those who crossed the Mediterranean alongside a rich understanding of the EU and member states' responses to this multi-faceted migration flow. In so doing, it provides a framework for understanding the dynamics underpinning recent unprecedented levels of migration across, and loss of life in, the Mediterranean. The book casts new light on the 'migration crisis' and challenges the public, politicians, policy makers and the media to rethink their understanding of why and how people move.

The need to rethink Europe's response has never been more pressing. The policies of the EU and its individual Member States reflect deep-seated and long-standing financial and political issues facing the Union (Crawley, 2016a; 2016b; Trauner, 2016). The response to increased migration across the Mediterranean has been disjointed, inconsistent and expensive. Billions of euros have been spent shoring up external and internal borders, often at the expense of a coherent, holistic, long-term response to the factors that drive migration in the first place (Cosgrove et al, 2016). The failures in relation to humanitarian assistance and longer-term integration have been increasingly well documented elsewhere (Amnesty International, 2015; 2016; 2017b; HRW, 2016a; Hernandez, 2016). Our focus here is specifically on EU policies related to the journeys that refugees and migrants took: the factors that caused them to leave; the reasons why they moved on from the countries to which they initially travelled; and their use of smugglers to access the protection to which many were entitled under international law.

Our research and evidence base

This book is based on data and analysis from a large-scale, systematic and comparative study – the MEDMIG project[3] – which explored the backgrounds, experiences, routes and aspirations of refugees and migrants who had recently arrived in three EU Member States – Italy, Greece and Malta – and Turkey (Crawley et al, 2016ab; McMahon and Sigona, 2016). Our overarching aim has been to better understand the processes which influence and inform migration. In particular we wanted our research to:

- shed light on the dynamics (determinants, drivers and infrastructures) underpinning the migration across the Mediterranean;
- provide insights into the interaction of refugees and migrants with a multitude of non-state actors, for example smugglers and civil society organisations (CSOs),[4] and state actors, for example politicians, policy makers and enforcement agencies (navy, coastguard and police), including how these interactions shaped their decision-making; and
- explore how the decisions made by refugees and migrants on their journeys were influenced by rapidly changing economic, security and policy contexts.

Our team of international researchers was based in Greece, Italy, Turkey and Malta from September 2015 to January 2016, when arrivals of women, men and children into the EU via southern Europe reached their peak. During this time, we interviewed 500 refugees and migrants: 205 people in Italy (Sicily, Apulia, Rome, Piedmont, Bologna) and 20 in Malta (Central Mediterranean route); 215 in Greece (Athens, Lesvos) and 60 in Turkey (Izmir, Istanbul) (Eastern Mediterranean route). The researchers employed a purposive sampling strategy to ensure that the backgrounds and demographic characteristics of respondents were broadly reflective of the larger population of people arriving in these countries during this time (Box 1.2).

We also interviewed over 100 stakeholders, including politicians, policy makers, naval officers and coastguards, representatives of international and local CSOs and volunteers. Stakeholder interviewees were selected for their ability to provide up-to-date information and contextual insight into the evolving migration flows and individual experiences in each location. The team also spent several months visiting many of the sites, observing 'the crisis' as it unfolded, and political and policy responses at the local, national and international levels.

The analysis in this book draws upon these interviews, together with our observations from the field and a desk-based review of the existing literature. Members of the research team have also been engaged in numerous national and international events (academic and practitioner seminars, public events, policy discussions, parliamentary inquiries and media debates) which have provided an opportunity to 'test out' some of our findings and ideas and to better understand the broader context within which our research was situated.[5]

Box 1.2: Our research sites

The choice of the countries in which the research was conducted – Greece, Italy, Turkey and Malta – reflects the key routes and locations of refugee and migrant arrivals to Europe during 2015. In each location we interviewed female and male refugees and migrants who were living inside formal reception centres as well as those who were living independently.

Our approach to the fieldwork had to be agile in order to adapt to rapidly changing contexts and events. We interviewed people who had only recently arrived as well as those who arrived earlier in 2015. In Greece, we found a chaotic context of arrival and reception from which refugees and migrants often sought to quickly move on (see Chapter Two). To adapt to this situation, interviews were carried out at the port of Mytilene on the island of Lesvos, which in numerical terms was the important place of arrival and transit to the Greek mainland. We also interviewed people at three locations in the city of Athens: Victoria Square where coaches departed for the Greek border with the Former Yugoslav Republic of Macedonia (FYROM), a second square where people were informally residing, and Eleonas camp, one of the first formal reception facilities in Athens.

In Italy, newly-arrived refugees and migrants were dispersed to state and non-governmental operated reception centres around the country (see Chapter Two). Many others quickly moved away from disembarkation locations or formal facilities on to other locations, choosing to live independently. We therefore carried out interviews in Eastern Sicily, Apulia and Piedmont, as well as in transit and reception centres in the cities of Rome and Bologna. In Malta our interviews were also conducted inside and outside formal reception facilities in Valetta and different locations on the island where refugees and migrants were living. Interviews in Turkey were conducted in Istanbul and in Izmir which, at that time, was the main hub for those seeking to move on to Greece.

The research generated a large data set within a very short period of time which was coded and analysed using NVivo to identify quantitative as well as qualitative patterns. This has enabled us to draw out broader patterns and trends within and across countries, different groups of refugees and migrants and according to demographic and other variables.

What this book does

While the focus of this book is on the stories and experiences of those who made the journey to Europe during 2015, we situate our analysis in the existing academic literature to inform – and make sense of – the complex and dynamic processes we found. We also draw on the findings of reports published since the beginning of 2015 by CSOs and others which have documented developments in the Mediterranean region (see, for example, Amnesty International, 2015; 2016; 2017a; HRW, 2015; MPI, 2015; MSF, 2016; UNHCR, 2015). Drawing on this data we challenge prevailing academic and policy understandings of Europe's 'migration crisis' in three important ways.

First, the book challenges assumptions about the linearity of refugee and migrant journeys to Europe. Much of the academic literature on migration to Europe has focused on the drivers of migration or on what happens to refugees and migrants when they reach countries of destination (see, for example, Thorburn, 1996; Castles et al, 2003; Neumayer, 2006). This tendency to neglect the 'in between' is reinforced by a body of academic literature on 'transit' migration which often presupposes that refugees and migrants who arrive in Europe are merely 'passing time' in other countries until opportunities for further onward migration arose (see also Collyer et al, 2012 for a critique of this idea). While some of our respondents made relatively short and direct journeys to Europe, the experiences of many others cannot accurately be described as singular 'journeys'. Rather they consisted of a series of consecutive movements, separated by often substantial periods (months, sometimes years) spent in one or more different locations in which they lived and worked with no intention of moving further (see also Collyer, 2010; Mainwaring and Brigden, 2016). Their onward movement, which was often in response to changing circumstances which undermined their security or ability to make a living, should be considered a separate migration decision.

Second, the book contributes to a more nuanced understanding of refugee and migrant decision making. We consider the ways in which a range of factors operating at the individual, societal and structural levels operate both independently of, and in relation to, one another to inform and shape people's decisions about whether to move and, if so, where to and when. Historically, much of the thinking around migration decision making has been dominated by push–pull models based on principles of utility maximisation, rational choice, factor–price differentials between regions and countries, and labour mobility. These models have been extensively critiqued as being overly simplistic and economically deterministic (King, 2012; Van Der Velde and Van Naerssen, 2015; EASO, 2016a). Not only do push–pull models make assumptions about the ways in which individuals respond to different factors, they presuppose that decisions are based on full information, neglect the role of intervening variables, and ignore or downplay a wide range of social factors, including social networks. The stories that refugees and migrants told us throw new light on the dynamics of migration towards, and across, the Mediterranean and challenge the assumptions on which migration policy making has been based.

Finally, the book challenges the tendency of academics, politicians and policy makers alike to use simplistic categories and dichotomies to differentiate between those on the move. There are few more challenging questions for academics and policy-makers than where, and how, to draw the line between 'forced' and 'voluntary' migration (Richmond, 1993; Zetter, 2007; Long, 2013; Betts, 2013; Carling, 2017; Crawley and Skleparis, 2017; McMahon and Sigona, forthcoming). The positioning of this line, and the factors, places and experiences which come to be associated with the categories that lie either side, shape our understanding of who constitutes a 'refugee' on the one hand, and an 'economic migrant' on the other. No less problematic is the idea that there is a clear-cut distinction between transit migration and immigration or between 'regular' and 'irregular' migration (Düvell, 2006; Bloch et al, 2011; Sigona and Hughes, 2012; Jansen et al, 2014).

The complex nature of contemporary global migration patterns presents huge challenges to existing international, regional and national legal and policy frameworks. This is partly because of the increasingly protracted and fragmented nature of journeys to Europe (Collyer, 2010). But it is also because migration policies are themselves pushing people into, and out of, categories which determine their access to protection and rights. For instance, people not immediately perceived as being 'refugees' because of their country of origin and may not receive the legal protection that they need. The current use of simplistic categories of 'forced' and 'voluntary' migration creates a two-tiered system of protection and assistance in which the rights and needs of those not qualifying as 'refugees' under the legal definition are effectively disregarded. It is important to challenge dominant, but mistaken, assumptions about who is or is not deserving of international protection.

The journey ahead

This book is about the dynamics of migration and the journeys and decisions of refugees and migrants, including the patterns of migration across the Mediterranean to Greece and Italy in 2015.

We set the scene in Chapter Two by providing a brief historical overview of Europe's so-called 'migration crisis'. Although there was, and continues to be, a tendency to talk about migration across the Mediterranean as a single, homogeneous flow, there were in fact two different and distinct routes. Not only was the scale and composition of migration into Italy and into Greece significantly different during 2015, so too were their governments' responses.

In Chapter Three we outline the characteristics of the 500 people we interviewed as part of our research, and document the routes they took before arriving in Europe. We also provide a framework for understanding the diverse array of strategies that individuals pursue in an attempt to secure safety and a livelihood for themselves and their families.

In Chapter Four we turn our attention to the factors that shaped the decision of our respondents to leave their home countries. We focus on the role of conflict, persecution and human rights abuses as well as on the complex and often overlapping relationship between 'forced' and 'economic' drivers of migration. We also examine where people wanted to go.

Chapter Five examines people's use of, and relationship with, the smugglers who facilitated the journey out of their countries of origin and into other countries including, ultimately, Europe. Like most other aspects of the story of Europe's 'migration crisis', the relationship between smugglers and those on the move is more complex than typically presented.

In Chapter Six we examine the decision making of those who spent extended periods of time in a number of other countries before arriving in Europe. These reasons included a lack of protection and security, the inability to find work or access services and the need for hope – and a sense of the future – for themselves and their families.

Chapter Seven takes the story to the shores of Europe with an account of people's journeys across the Mediterranean and what happened when they arrived. For most respondents this was not the end of the story. But while politicians and the media focused on the onwards movements of people up through the Balkans to the countries of northern Europe, our research has identified other movements taking place about which much less was heard.

We conclude in Chapter Eight by reflecting on the EU's response to increased migration across the Mediterranean in 2015. This response has largely failed to address either the drivers of migration to Europe or the needs of refugees and migrants arriving on Europe's shores. Moreover it has, we argue, contributed to the perception of migration as a 'crisis'. The EU requires a much more nuanced response which is underpinned by an understanding of the factors that drive people to leave their homes and lead them to move on. The insights this book provides into the dynamics of migration across the Mediterranean during 2015 will, we hope, inform this new approach.

Notes

[1] All names are pseudonyms to protect the identity of respondents.

[2] We use the term 'refugees and migrants' throughout this book to reflect the nature of 'mixed flows' across the Mediterranean and the movement of people between categories across time and space (see also Crawley and Skleparis, 2017).

[3] The MEDMIG project was led by the Centre for Trust, Peace and Social Relations at Coventry University, in collaboration with the University of Birmingham (UK), the University of Oxford (UK), ELIAMEP (Greece), FIERI (Italy), People for Change Foundation (Malta) and Yasar University (Turkey). More information about the project can be found at www.medmig.info MEDMIG was part of the Mediterranean Migration Research Programme (MMRP) established through the Economic and Social Research Council's (ESRC) £1 million 'Urgency Grant', co-funded by the UK's Department for International Development (DfID). More information about MMRP can be found at http://www2.warwick.ac.uk/fac/soc/mmrp/

[4] This book uses the term CSO to include all non-market and non-state organisations outside of the family in which people organise themselves to pursue shared interests in the public domain. CSOs include a diverse set of organisations, ranging from small, informal, community-based organisations to the large, high-profile, INGOs working through local partners. CSOs, by their very nature, are independent of direct government control and management.

[5] Details of these events can be found on our project website www.medmig. info

TWO

Unravelling Europe's 'migration crisis'

Before unpacking the journeys of the refugees and migrants with whom we spoke, we need to first situate the 'migration crisis' within its wider geographical and historical context. This is important because it suggests that the 'crisis' was neither singular in the way that it unfolded at the EU southern borders, nor one of numbers *per se*. Migration across the Mediterranean was not new and irregular boat crossings, particularly along the Central and Western Mediterranean routes,[1] have attracted attention since the 1990s. Neither should the rise in sea arrivals have been unexpected given events that had been unfolding in the region since 2011, most notably in Libya and Syria. However, while Italy had put in place a set of urgency measures since 2011, Greece was unprepared for the rapid and sudden increase in spontaneous sea arrivals. The failure to provide appropriate reception facilities for refugees and migrants arriving in increasingly large numbers in the summer of 2015 led to chaotic scenes on the Greek islands, a humanitarian crisis unlike that seen previously and an overwhelming sense that the situation was 'out of control'. This perception was exacerbated by dramatic images of tens of thousands of people moving onwards through Europe.

Mediterranean migration in global and historical context

Migration across the Mediterranean generated endless media coverage and political discussion during 2015. Yet, arrivals were not particularly large when compared with migratory flows in other regions of the world, or even migration into and across Europe at other times in history.

First, migration to Europe has to be understood in the context of global migration flows. Although the percentage of the world's population living outside their country of origin has not changed significantly in the last few decades, the number of international migrants has increased by 41% since 2000, in part due to the rapid increase in the world's population (UN, 2015a). Globally, employment and family reunification remain the main reasons for migration but conflict, persecution and human rights abuse has also forced more people to leave their homes than ever before. By the end of 2015 more than 65 million people were displaced worldwide, one third of whom (21.3 million) were refugees living outside their countries of origin (UNHCR, 2016): the remainder were internally displaced. What is important is that the scale of displacement accelerated during the course of 2015 with an estimated 12.4 million people newly displaced due to conflict or persecution during the course of the year. These figures remained largely unchanged in 2016 (UNHCR, 2017a).

Some countries have been particularly affected by forced migration. The conflict in the Syrian Arab Republic (Syria) began in March 2011 but escalated during the course of 2014 and 2015. By early 2016, more than 11% of the country's population had either died or been injured.[2] At the time of writing, two thirds of the population of Syria has been displaced: Syria is the only country in which the experience of displacement now affects the majority of the population (UNHCR, 2017a). Many other conflicts also contributed to the increased global displacement figures during 2015. These included new or reignited conflicts in Burundi, Iraq, Libya, Niger and Nigeria, together with older or unresolved crises in Afghanistan, the Central African Republic, the Democratic Republic of the Congo, South Sudan, Somalia and Yemen (see HRW, 2016a). Ongoing political persecution in countries such as Eritrea and Gambia also displaced large numbers of people (OHCHR, 2015; UNHCR, 2016).

Second, while the number of people who arrived in Europe across the Mediterranean was significantly higher than in previous years and occurred over a short space of time, it nonetheless represented just a small proportion of those who were forcibly displaced around the world in 2015. Of those who left their countries in search of protection, the vast majority (86%) fled to neighbouring, mostly low and middle income countries (UNHCR, 2016). In other words, the brunt of hosting people displaced by conflict has been borne by neighbouring countries, not Europe.

Finally, it is worth noting that 2015 was not the first time that significant numbers of people were displaced within Europe. The end of the Second World War brought in its wake the largest population movements in European history as millions of Germans fled or were expelled from Eastern Europe (Douglas, 2015). During the suppression of the uprising that took place in Hungary in October 1956, some 180,000 Hungarians fled to Austria and another 20,000 to Yugoslavia. Then, in the early 1990s, more than three million people were forced to leave towns and villages in the Federal Republic of Yugoslavia (FRY) after it began to disintegrate in 1991 (Barutciski, 1994; Roch, 1995). Moreover, the arrival of people across the Mediterranean has characterised Europe's history and has featured strongly in political and policy debates at various points in time over the past 25 years (see, for example, Lutterbeck, 2006; de Haas, 2008). These movements did not generate the same sense of 'crisis' seen in relation to more recent boat migration to Italy and Greece.

Boat migration to Italy and Greece

Italy and Greece have quite different histories when it comes to the arrival of refugees and migrants by boat (Figure 2.1). While rarely acknowledged in the story of Europe's 'migration crisis', boat migration from North Africa has been a seasonal feature in Italy and Malta since at least the 1990s. Since 2010, it has steadily increased while retaining

Figure 2.1: Arrivals into Italy and Greece, May 2013 to July 2017[3]

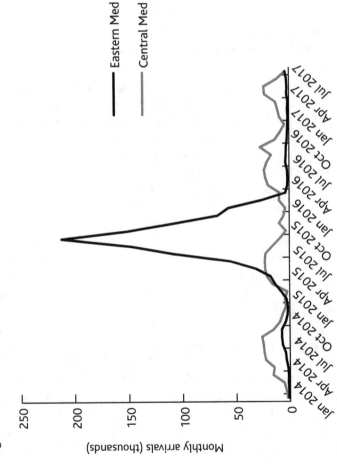

a similar pattern to previous years. The number of people arriving in Italy in 2015 was, however, actually *lower* not higher than the previous year (IOM, 2016a). In Greece, by contrast, there have historically been more limited arrivals by sea. Here the rapid increase in the arrivals of refugees and migrants in 2015 reflected the 'coming together' of a number of different factors both in Syria and in the countries to which people initially fled.

While in 2014 most people had crossed to Europe from Libya into Italy, the majority (84%) of those arriving by boat in 2015 entered Europe through Greece from departure points dotted along the Turkish coast. During the course of the year, the story of Europe's 'migration crisis' shifted from a focus on the hundreds of people drowning in the Mediterranean between Libya and Italy to the arrival of thousands of people each day in Greece. In October 2015 more than 210,000 people arrived on the Greek islands, a remarkable increase on the 7,432 whose arrival was recorded 12 months earlier. But as we explain in more detail below, it was not just these shifts in the number of arrivals that underlay the perception of a 'migration crisis': the other significant, and related, difference between the two routes concerns the way in which people arrived, with so-called spontaneous arrivals *de facto* disappearing from the Central Mediterranean route because of the implementation of search and rescue (SAR) operations, which both saved lives at sea and enabled an orderly disembarkation in Italian ports.

Arrivals in Italy and Malta

Although the scale of migration to Italy by boat has increased since 2010, this route has been used by refugees and migrants seeking to reach Europe for many years. In the early 1990s many people made the journey across the Adriatic by boat from Albania to Apulia, perhaps most memorably with the arrival of thousands crammed onto the *Vlora*, the cargo ship which arrived in the port of Bari in August 1991 (Frenzen, 2011). Although Italian and European authorities had considerably less capacity to detect and record journeys compared with

Figure 2.2: Arrivals across the Central Mediterranean route to Italy and Malta, 2005–16[4]

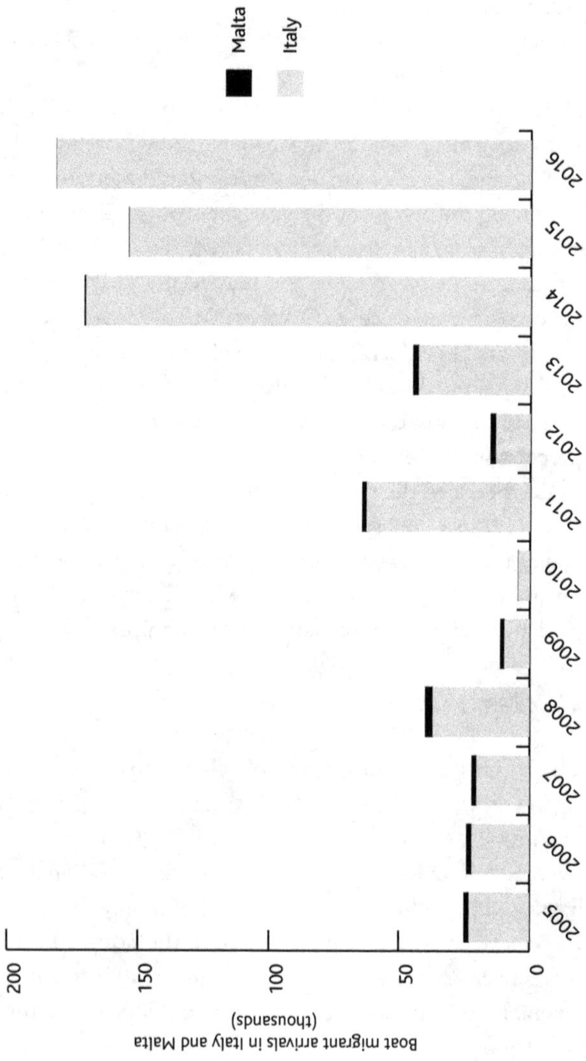

today, an average of 23,000 migrants were counted travelling to Italy by boat each year between 1997 and 2010 (McMahon and Sigona, 2016).[5]

The dynamics of increased movement across the Mediterranean to Italy are closely intertwined with the medium- to long-term evolution of international migration to and from North Africa, and particularly Libya (Box 2.1). The increase in number of people arriving in Italy in 2011 resulted from the political instability which followed the Arab Spring when protests for rights and democracy swept across many countries of North Africa and the Middle East. As governments in Tunisia and Egypt fell and military repression, armed insurrection and protracted conflict took hold in Libya, many fled on boats across the Mediterranean to Italy. This included not only nationals of the affected countries, but also refugees and migrants from elsewhere who had been living in these countries. The significant increase in people arriving in 2014 occurred as Libya descended into a renewed and especially chaotic civil war. Today, the various militias and tribal factions throughout the country are said to profit from migrant smuggling into, through and out of the country (Micallef, 2017).

The profile of arrivals in Italy in 2015 was markedly different from Greece, both in terms of national origins and size: the top five nationalities in 2015 were Eritreans, Nigerians, Gambians, Somali and Sudanese which together accounted for 59% of arrivals (IOM, 2016a). Syrian nationals, who in 2014 were among the top five nationalities arriving, accounted for just 5% in 2015. The diversity of arrivals across the Central Mediterranean route is noteworthy.

Box 2.1: The deteriorating situation in Libya

In February 2011 the security forces of Muammar Gaddafi responded to protests for democracy by using force, opening fire on protesters in the city of Benghazi. Soon after, armed groups started to fight back. The UN Security Council called for the protection of civilians and a no-fly zone was enforced by western governments by carrying out strikes on military targets in the country. By August of the same year Gaddafi was dead and the regime defeated.

Hope for unity and a transition to peace underpinned the first elections in a post-Gaddafi Libya, which were held in July 2012. Since then 'almost everything has gone awry' (Toaldo, 2014, 2). Despite a strong popular turnout during the 2012 elections, tensions and battles for political and economic power continued among a wide range of armed groups across the country. In elections for a Constitution Drafting Assembly to shape the country's political institutions which took place in February 2014, popular turnout was only 15% as people lost hope in the country finding a new direction (Toaldo, 2014).

Many armed groups and militias had formed across the country in the fight against Gaddafi's regime. They were usually based in their own particular towns or cities. In the post-Gaddafi era, there has been little progress in uniting them and in many cases they have continued to provide local security and governance systems over their territories. Furthermore, other armed groups have staked a claim to political power in different parts of the country since 2012. Former oil facility guards established an independent government in the East, while ethnic minority and tribal groups in the south and Jihadi groups in the East and in Tripoli continued fighting. This chaotic situation was described in early 2015 as making Libya a country 'divided between three rival governments and dozens of armed groups' (Toaldo, 2015).

The instability and fighting among these groups has severely affected the country's economy and society. Lawless neighbourhoods exist across the country (Micallef, 2017). In addition to benefiting from trafficking in arms and oil, militia groups have also allegedly (but not surprisingly) recently taken over migrant smuggling networks and migrant detention facilities.

Malta, by contrast, has only seen annual arrivals of on average just under 1,600 people over the past decade, with peaks in 2008 (2,775) and 2013 (2,008) but then declining sharply to 568 in 2014 and 104 in 2015. In 2016 there were only 25 arrivals by boat, and these were all urgent medical cases. The low number of people arriving in Malta is striking given that search and rescue (SAR) operations carried out by the Malta-based Maritime Offshore Aid Station (MOAS) have saved over 30,000 people since 2014. However, in 2015 an agreement was reached between Italy and Malta that those rescued would, in future, be disembarked at Italian ports. This arrangement was the subject of political and public interest, with accusations of a secret pact between

Malta and Italy in which Malta would surrender oil exploration rights in an offshore area disputed with Italy, while Italy would return the favour by picking up Malta's share of refugees and migrants rescued at sea.[6]

Arrivals to Greece from Turkey

Historically, most irregular migrants to Greece have originated from neighbouring Albania or Eastern European countries and have arrived overland or by plane rather than by boat (Psimmenos and Kassimati, 2006). In 2015, the majority of people arrived on the small island of Lesvos (population of 86,000), with smaller numbers of people arriving on Kos, Chios and Samos (Figure 2.2). According to UNHCR (2016) over half (56%) of the 850,000 people arriving in Greece by sea in 2015 were of Syrian nationality (or of Palestinian origin living in Syria), followed by Afghans travelling either from Afghanistan or Iran (24%), and Iraqis (10%). The remainder was composed of relatively small numbers coming from a significant number of countries (74 in total) (IOM, 2016a). Given that 85% of those arriving in Europe during 2015 came via this route, Europe's so-called 'migration crisis' can be more accurately described as a crisis of refugee protection, a point to which we will return.

It is only possible to understand the sudden, and largely unexpected, increase in boat arrivals to Greece in 2015 by looking at the situation in Syria and events that had unfolded in the region since the start of the conflict in 2011, and, in particular, the actions of Syria's neighbours in closing their borders, as well as the actions of the Greek government in closing their land border with Turkey.

Despite, or perhaps because of, the conflict that gripped Syria from March 2011 onwards, the borders surrounding the country gradually closed over the period 2013–15, first to Palestinian Syrians and latterly to all Syrians. As a result, the options for those deciding to leave Syria, where the conflict showed no signs of abating, were becoming increasingly limited. In the case of Lebanon, visa restrictions including a restriction of categories by which Syrians could enter, new

Figure 2.3: Arrivals to Greece across the Eastern Mediterranean route, January to December 2015[7]

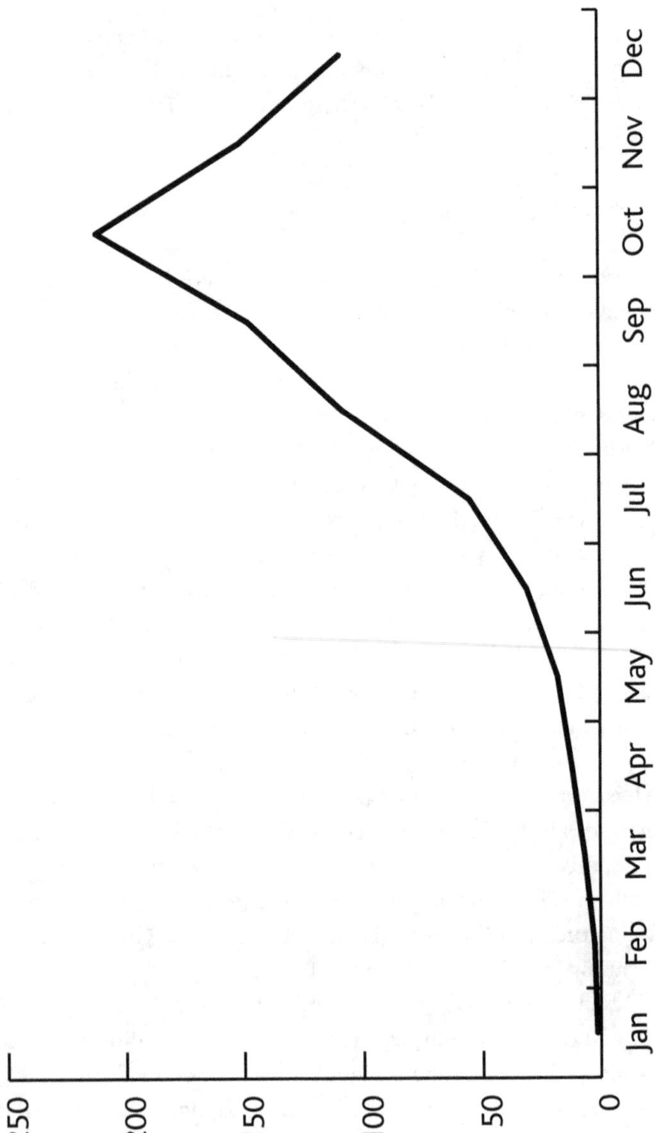

requirements of a Lebanese sponsor and fees of up to US$200 were imposed in October 2014, December 2014 and April 2015 so that by May 2015 the border was effectively closed to all but the richest and most well-connected. Meanwhile Jordan, which had played host to a significant number of Syrian refugees, began closing informal and formal border crossings to Syrians from 2013. In May 2014 Jordan officially barred entry at Amman's Queen Alia International Airport to all Syrians without Jordanian residency permits or special exceptions.[8] During 2014 and 2015, the North African states (Algeria, Egypt, Morocco and Tunisia) also imposed visa restrictions, deporting and detaining some of those Syrians already in the countries. European governments also began restricting access to visas for Syrians. In the UK, for example, the refusal rate for Syrians stood at 58% in 2015 compared with 32% before the conflict began.[9]

Border closures reducing the opportunities for safe and legal travel out of Syria, combined with increased fighting in the north west of Syria (the areas closest to the Turkish border) and increasing territorial gains by Islamic State (IS), funnelled people towards Turkey. In the period from 2011 to 2015 more than 2.5 million people fled across the border from neighbouring Syria, making Turkey the largest host country for refugees worldwide for the last three years (UNHCR, 2016; 2017a) (Box 2.2).

Up until 2012, irregular migrants entering Greece from Turkey entered mostly by the land border in Thrace and the Edirne region and across the Evros river. However, in 2011–12, the Greek government constructed a 6.5km fence bordering the Evros which effectively closed its land border. The numbers entering Greece through this route consequently fell by 90%, while the numbers crossing the Aegean by boat to the Greek islands located close to Turkey rose considerably from 2012 to 2013, and even more so from 2014 (Angeli et al, 2014).

Box 2.2: Migration flows to Turkey

Historically, Turkey has always been an important destination country for refugees and migrants, including from Bulgaria, the former Yugoslavia, former Soviet Union countries, Iraq and elsewhere. Already from the mid to late 1990s, Turkey had also become a country through which refugees and migrants transited on their way to Europe: from 1996 to 2010, around a million people were apprehended in Turkey, usually on exit. However, from around 2010, Turkey went through a migration transition meaning that as a result of its economic growth, relative political stability, heightened demand for migrant labour and a liberal visa regime, it became a net immigration country for people from a wide range of backgrounds including business people, workers, retirees, students and refugees (Düvell, 2014a). In 2011, when the Syrian people began protesting against the Assad regime, very few fled the country: it was the government backlash from 2012 that triggered the first significant displacement and most of these people escaped to Jordan and Lebanon. But as the borders in the regions closed, the number of Syrian refugees moving to Turkey increased. By mid-2014, Turkey hosted around one million refugees: by summer 2015, this rose to 1.7 million, 2.7 million by early 2016 and up to 3 million in May 2017. In addition, Turkey received another 200,000–300,000 refugees from Iraq, Afghanistan, Iran and other countries (DGMM, 2016a).

The international community's response was largely inadequate. As early as 2014, concerns were raised that the countries hosting Syrian refugees in the region were seriously underfunded (Spijkerboer, 2016). As is clear from the stories of those we spoke to during our research, life for Syrians and other refugees living in Turkey became increasingly difficult during 2014 and 2015. But many of those crossing the Aegean from Turkey to Greece had moved initially to Jordan and Lebanon where life had become even more uncertain. In December 2014 the World Food Programme suspended food aid to more than 1.7 million Syrian refugees for lack of funding, predicting that this would have 'disastrous' results.[10] And so it proved to be.

Diverging policy responses

Against the backdrop of a narrative of Europe's 'migration crisis' as a singular and undifferentiated phenomenon, this brief overview of the profile of sea arrivals in Italy and Greece in 2015 and the respective governments' experience of handling irregular boat migration highlights significant differences between the two main routes. To understand the politics of the crisis, however, the different political contexts at the time should also be considered.

Since 2013 Italy had been led by centre-left governments with a more humanitarian, if not pro-immigration, agenda to that seen previously in the country (McMahon, 2017). This was a noticeable change from the previous Berlusconi government which had made Lampedusa an icon of the migrant 'invasion'. Greece, by contrast, was still deeply affected by the economic and financial crisis and the austerity measures imposed by the EU. Social and political unrest and unprecedented levels of unemployment meant that the country was unprepared to cope with sea arrivals and responded at a slower pace to the rapidly changing scenario. In addition, the Greek asylum system had been subject to criticism from UNHCR and others long before arrivals increased in 2015. Most notably, in 2011 the EU's Court of Justice ruled that asylum seekers could not be returned to Greece under Dublin Regulation III[11] due to systematic deficiencies in the asylum procedures and in reception conditions (see also UNHCR, 2014).[12] The diverging responses of the Greek and Italian governments to the arrival of refugees and migrants provides an important backdrop to the story of Europe's 'migration crisis' and is one to which we will return in Chapter Eight.

As thousands of people arrived on Italian shores in early 2011, Italy announced the 'Emergenza Nordafrica'. This was associated with the rapid expansion of the capacity of the Italian reception system and monitoring of boats at sea. Following the 2013 Lampedusa tragedy, in which hundreds of people drowned, the Italian navy implemented extensive patrolling of the international waters and carried out thousands of SAR operations under the auspices of the

Mare Nostrum operation (discussed further in Chapter Eight). By intercepting boats at sea, Italy implemented a policy of 'managed disembarkations'. This meant that people were, for the most part, rescued at sea, and taken to Italian ports in the rescue vessels. As a result, so-called 'spontaneous arrivals' almost disappeared. The Italian government has increasingly sought to contain migrants in order to ease their identification, categorisation and relocation either within Italy, to other EU Member States or back to countries of origin and transit. At the ports a first identification process would take place, registering names, ages, nationalities, gender and so on before transfers were made either to reception facilities for refugees and asylum seekers or to expulsion centres. This managed approach kept boat arrivals largely out of public sight and moderated the narrative of 'invasion' which had dominated political and media discourse until that point. Nevertheless, after a year of Mare Nostrum (October 2013–14), the policy objective of preventing further boat migration regained primacy in the political debate as the newly appointed PM Matteo Renzi called for closer involvement of the EU in what he repeatedly depicted as a 'European problem'.[13]

The managed arrival of refugees and migrants in Italy stood in stark contrast to the situation in Greece, where large numbers of people arriving spontaneously on the Greek islands led to chaotic scenes on the beaches. Shortly after taking power in 2015, the incoming Greek government under the Prime Ministership of Alex Tsipras announced that the previous policy of detaining all irregular migrants was to be abandoned, partly in an effort to move the new government away from the highly restrictive and extensively criticised policies which had been a feature of the previous government. In March 2015 an official document was leaked which stated that refugees and migrants entering the country irregularly would not be detained at the borders but would instead be provided with a document which instructed them to leave the country in 30 days. This was widely viewed as an unofficial 'travel document' enabling people to transit through Greece. However, as the numbers arriving on the islands increased throughout the summer of 2015, the lack of preparation and lack of facilities became more apparent.

During the summer of 2015 and onwards, provision of reception facilities and other services by international organisations and NGOs in Greece sprung up largely in a void of state-led emergency provision. By the autumn, refugees and migrants arriving on Greek beaches were increasingly met by a mixture of volunteers, CSO representatives and journalists who provided them with food, water, information and sometimes transportation to the first reception camp. The relative lack of involvement of the Greek government (both nationally and on the islands) was partly a consequence of the political instability which had been generated by the austerity crisis and challenging negotiations with the EU over its financial 'bail-out'. But it also reflected a flawed assumption that if the government 'did nothing' this would deter people from coming to Greece, or from staying if they did (Skleparis, 2017). At the same time, the central government effectively promoted quick onward migration to the rest of the EU, even persuading the neighbouring Former Yugoslav Republic of Macedonia (FYROM) to open the borders, in order to avoid providing either meaningful access to international protection or reception facilities and integration opportunities that would enable people to stay while their claims were determined. As we will see in the chapters that follow, this approach resulted not only in significant human misery for those arriving in Europe but a growing sense of 'crisis' from which the EU is still struggling to recover.

Notes

[1] The Western Mediterranean route from Morocco to Spain route had been a noted entry point since 2005, when thousands of refugees and migrants made headlines by trying to climb over the fence in the Spanish enclave of Melilla.

[2] This figure is from a report published by the Syrian Centre for Policy Research, www.scpr-syria.org, which was widely reported by the international press, see, for example, www.pbs.org/wgbh/frontline/article/a-staggering-new-death-toll-for-syrias-war-470000/

[3] Data from Frontex, available at http://frontex.europa.eu/trends-and-routes/migratory-routes-map/

[4] Based on data from UNHCR, Italian data at http://data.unhcr.org/mediterranean and Maltese data at www.unhcr.org.mt/charts/category/12

[5] Data from UNHCR at http://data.unhcr.org/mediterranean

[6] More at http://uk.businessinsider.com/italy-and-malta-accused-of-trading-oil-for-refugees-2016-4

[7] Data from UNHCR, http://data.unhcr.org/mediterranean

[8] Human Rights Watch (2015) 'Jordan: Syrians blocked, stranded in desert', 3 June, www.hrw.org/news/2015/06/03/jordan-syrians-blocked-stranded-desert

[9] Yeo, C. (2015) 'Refusal rate for Syrian visa applications increases yet further', www.freemovement.org.uk/refusal-rate-for-syrian-visa-applications-increases-yet-further/

[10] Frontline (2014) '1.7 million Syrian refugees to lose their main source of food aid' 1 December, www.pbs.org/wgbh/frontline/article/1-7-million-syrian-refugees-to-lose-their-main-source-of-food-aid/

[11] The Dublin III Regulation (Regulation 604/2013) entered into force on 1 January 2014 and sets down the criteria and the mechanisms of determination of the Member State in charge of examining the request of international protection presented by a third-country national or by a stateless person in one of the European states. This basically means that the Dublin III Regulation defines which State has the obligation to evaluate the asylum request presented by people who arrive in Europe. This is normally the first EU Member State in which an individual arrives. More information about the Dublin Regulation can be found at https://openmigration.org/en/analyses/what-is-the-dublin-regulation/

[12] See Court of Justice of the European Union, Press Release No. 140/11, Luxembourg, 21 December 2011 'An asylum seeker may not be transferred to a Member State where he risks being subjected to inhuman treatment', www.europa.eu/rapid/press-release_CJE-11-140_en.pdf

[13] Although this was not a new depiction: in 2011 the first large-scale arrivals of people on Lampedusa were also described as a problem for Europe (McMahon, 2012).

THREE

Not one route but many: unpacking migration to Europe

Although migration across the Mediterranean in 2015 was often discussed as if it was a single flow it was, as we have seen, composed of two routes – one to Italy, one to Greece – which were themselves a product of the merging of multiple flows which converged in Libya and Turkey respectively. Each of these flows was, in turn, composed of people with different characteristics and different migratory experiences. This chapter outlines the characteristics of the refugees and migrants we spoke to during our research before describing the routes and journeys that they took prior to their arrival in Europe. These included not only the journey to Europe itself but also longer-term trajectories and serial migration decisions which involve what we refer to as 'stops' and 'stays' of varying duration, often with no predetermined final destination.

Who was on the move?

There were significant differences between the Eastern and Central Mediterranean routes not only in terms of the scale and history of migration flows but also in terms of the composition of people making the different sea crossings during 2015. While 90% of those arriving in Greece came from just three countries (Syria, Afghanistan and Iraq), arrivals in Italy were much more diverse: around a quarter of all arrivals were Eritrean (25.5%), followed by Nigerians (14.5%), Somalis (8.1%), Sudanese (5.8%), Gambians (5.8%) and Syrians (3.8%), with the remainder originating from 53 different countries (IOM, 2016a).

While we do not claim our data to be completely representative, the sample of people interviewed is one of the largest of its kind and broadly reflects the composition of those arriving in Greece and Italy in 2015. In Greece the largest proportion originated from Syria (44.5%), followed by Afghanistan (20.5%) and Iraq (13.5%) (see Figure 3.1). In Italy, our sample mirrors the marked diversity of countries of origin among sea arrivals (see Figure 3.2).

Figure 3.1: Nationality of respondents interviewed in Greece (215 respondents)

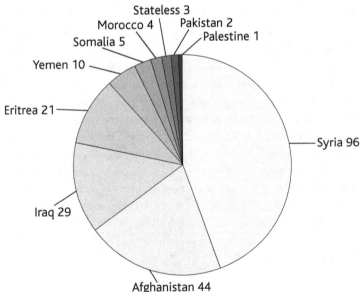

Figure 3.2: Nationality of respondents interviewed in Italy (205 respondents)

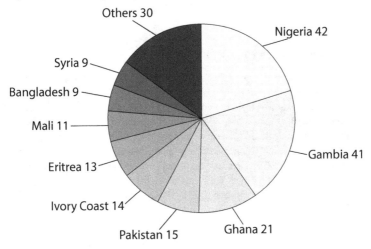

There were also differences in terms of age, gender and whether people were travelling with their children in each of the case study countries, some of which reflected broader trends. Just over two-thirds (65%) of those interviewed were aged 18–29 but the proportion was higher in Italy (76.5%) than in Greece (54.5%). This reflects the fact that those arriving in Greece were more likely to be older and travelling in family groups. Across the sample as a whole, 38% had children and, of these, 25% were travelling with their children. However, the proportion of people travelling with children was significantly higher on the Eastern Mediterranean route compared with the Central Mediterranean route. In the latter stages of our fieldwork in Greece respondents also referred more frequently to family members already in Northern Europe. By contrast, although around a third (30%) of those travelling from North Africa to Italy and Malta had children, the vast majority (88.5%) of them had left their children behind in their countries of origin, usually with other family members.

There is a low proportion of women in the sample. This is partly because men were more likely to make the long and risky journey to Europe than women. But it also reflects the fact that men more commonly put themselves forward to be interviewed about their family's experiences when travelling with wives, daughters and mothers.

Box 3.1: Children in Europe's 'migration crisis'

Children travelling with their families across the Mediterranean to Europe are often invisible in data and policy (Humphris and Sigona, 2016). It is estimated that around 250,000 arrived in 2015, with the vast majority (94%) arriving in Greece (UNHCR, 2016). A closer look at the data on children arriving in Greece and Italy shows remarkable differences in their countries of origin, and whether the children travelled with family members or alone. The overwhelming majority of children from Egypt (98%) and Gambia (96%) travelled alone on the treacherous sea crossing from North Africa. The opposite was the case for the Syrian children and young people. Afghans under the age of 18 years were also more likely to arrive on their own.

These broad patterns are reflected in the composition of the sample of people interviewed for this research. We interviewed a total of 73 adults (on their own and in couples) who travelled across the Mediterranean with their children, of whom 47 were interviewed in Greece, six in Italy and 20 in Turkey. The presence of children at home, or on the journey, influenced migrant decision making and perceptions of risk and opportunity. Parents were aware of the duress of the journey for their children but weighed these risks against those associated with staying put. Lack of educational opportunities, children's personal safety and aspirations for their future were also cited as factors influencing the decision to stay put or move on.

Refugees and migrants arriving in Greece during 2015 were generally better-educated and from higher socio-economic groups than those arriving in Italy. Overall, two-thirds of our respondents had a secondary school or university education but for those arriving in Greece this rose to 78%. Most people arriving in Greece also had a job before making the journey (91%). In Italy, the figure was 57%. This was most likely a reflection of the countries from which our respondents originated and the corresponding opportunities that had previously been available to them.

Regions and routes

Before beginning our discussion of regions and routes, it should be noted that there was huge diversity in the journeys made by the men and women who participated in this research, not only in the countries to which they had travelled and the time spent there, but also the extent of regular and irregular movement in each place. Refugees and migrants who had crossed the Mediterranean had usually travelled along multiple and varying routes prior to their arrival in Europe, mostly making use of the same infrastructure (dirt tracks, roads, buses, ferries, planes) available to other travellers. They had travelled through a wide range of countries prior to their arrival in Europe, stretching across diverse areas of the world and, in some extreme cases, even taking in countries in Southern Africa, the Americas and East Asia. Although there were two main countries from which refugees and migrants departed towards Europe, namely Turkey and Libya, the 'back story' to this migration was actually composed of an intricate network of varied routes crossing the different regions from which refugees and migrants had originated.

Overall, the 500 people we interviewed had passed through a total of 57 different countries. On the Eastern Mediterranean route, they had travelled through a total of 21 different countries prior to reaching Greece, comprising a total of 26 geographical routes. On the Central Mediterranean route there was even greater variation, with refugees and migrants having crossed 36 different countries before reaching Italy or Malta and describing a total of 68 different routes through them. Furthermore, the Central and Eastern Mediterranean routes were not entirely separate and distinct. In addition to the two main routes in the Central Mediterranean and the Eastern Mediterranean we identified 20 people in Italy (mostly, Pakistanis, some Syrians and one Bengali) who had actually travelled via Turkey and Greece. A further three respondents in Malta, all Syrians, had also travelled via the Eastern Mediterranean route. We discuss these movements in more detail in Chapter Six.

Altogether, our respondents had made more than 3,000 stops, equating to an average of six stops per person between their country of origin and the location of our interview with them in Italy, Malta or Greece. Among the locations of these stops, we identified a number of 'hubs' in which goods and services, including those needed for settlement or onward travel, were accessed by respondents (Box 2.2). These included Tehran and Urmia (Iran), Van, Istanbul and Izmir (Turkey), Lesvos and Athens (Greece), Kassala and Khartoum (Sudan), Bamako (Mali), Niamey and Agadez (Niger), Sabha, Tripoli and Zuwarah (Libya), and Rome (Italy). Others had also stopped elsewhere within Europe, either during periods of previous settlement in places such as France or Germany or when travelling through Greece, Italy or the Balkans to reach other destinations. And yet, despite the extremely diverse patterns and routes taken by our respondents, their journeys ultimately converged at the Mediterranean to form more or less discernible flows to Europe via the Eastern and Central sea crossings.

Box 3.2: Agadez and Izmir as migration 'hubs'

Agadez (Central Mediterranean route)

Against the backdrop of multiple diverse migration routes and patterns between Africa and Europe, the town of Agadez in Niger stands out. It represented a key stopping point between Central and North Africa for many of the people we spoke to. No fewer than 87 people from West and Central African countries (55% of the total) who crossed to Italy had, at some point, travelled through Agadez. This particular location is therefore an important focal point for our understanding of the dynamics of migration towards, and across, the Mediterranean to Europe.

Agadez sits at the southern end of the Sahara Desert. During the time of our research, it was the place from which the majority of the journeys towards Libya across the desert departed. Bus routes from Bamako in Mali or Ouagadougou in Burkina Faso ended here, with onward travel organised by smugglers using pickup trucks and lorries. This was nothing new: Agadez has been the departure point for journeys through the desert for many years. It was even a hub for tourist expeditions in the Sahara for the 1980s and 1990s, with diaries from those expeditions noting that trucks loaded with contraband and West African workers were already passing along the same route across the desert in 2000. Goods were transported into

Libya, particularly during times of sanctions against Gaddafi's government, and weapons and munitions brought back to be sold in Niger and Mali. IOM recorded over 60,000 refugees and migrants passing through Agadez between February and April 2016 alone.[1] At the time of our research, the town's economy was said to be almost entirely based on providing services of one kind or another to refugees and migrants, including smuggling services. As a result, it was not difficult to find a person known as a 'connection man', who could organise the onward journey. In fact, 'connection men' would be touting their services openly to people as they arrived.

Izmir (Eastern Mediterranean route)

The Turkish city of Izmir, on the Aegean coast in the west of the country, is home to almost three million people and both an economic and tourist hub. During 2015 it also became known as key site from where people were taken to the coasts of Ayvacik, Ayvalik, Cesme, Kusadasi or Bodrum in order to cross the Aegean to Greece. Historically, Izmir has been an important destination for internal migrants, usually from eastern Turkey. It was also an important arrival and host city for Syrian refugees with over 111,000 officially registered at the time of our research (DGMM, 2016a). And it was a departure city: a significant proportion of people travelling to Europe via the Eastern Mediterranean route mentioned Izmir as a place through which they travelled, often staying in the Basmane district, an old inner-city quarter by a major train station which offered all the services travellers needed. The district has previously been identified as an important transit hub for those on their route across Turkey to Europe (Wissink et al, 2013).

During our research in Basmane we found a bustling neighbourhood offering a variety of services to refugees and migrants: a mixed economy of hotels and smugglers, or rather their middlemen, as well as businesses catering for the needs of refugees and migrants including diverse shops, cafes and barbers often advertising their services in Arabic. Some shops sold inflatable dinghies, outboard engines, life-vests and water-proof document bags for use on the sea crossing to Greece. In addition, local mosques offered shelter and meals while CSOs provided clothes, non-food items, and services such as counselling. By late summer 2015 these activities had even spread into neighbouring, more upmarket, districts surrounding Basmane.

The Eastern Mediterranean route

All of those interviewed in Greece had travelled through, and thus departed from, Turkey. However, prior to the Mediterranean crossing, distinct routes to Turkey were in evidence, each composed of various 'legs'. People coming from countries which bordered Turkey (Syria, Iraq and Iran) generally undertook journeys which were relatively straightforward: women, men and family groups crossed land borders into Turkey, often from Syria to towns such as Kilis and Gaziantep. From Iran, people mostly travelled clandestinely towards the border, crossing the more dangerous mountain border on foot to arrive in the Van region of Turkey. From Kilis, Gaziantep and Van they travelled onwards to the coast via Ankara, Istanbul and Antakya. By contrast, journeys from further afield in the Middle East, Africa or the Gulf could involve air, land or ferry travel according to the resources and opportunities available to the person making the journey.

In summary, we were able to identify three principal routes which converged in Turkey and thus contributed to the significant increase in arrivals to Greece during the course of 2015:

- *a neighbourhood route*, from Syria, Iraq and Iran into Turkey and then from the southern border region via Istanbul, Ankara, or Mersin and Adana towards Izmir and then on to the Greek islands;
- *a Middle Eastern regional route*, from Afghanistan and sometimes Pakistan or through Iran into Eastern Turkey (Van), or from Lebanon overland or by ferry to Southern Turkey (Gaziantep, Antakya, Mersin), and via Ankara and/or Istanbul to the Aegean coast;
- *a Middle Eastern and North African (mostly MENA) route* from Sudan, Egypt, Somalia, Egypt, Morocco and Tunisia or the Gulf countries (UAE, Oman) into Turkey, continuing on as above.

The Central Mediterranean route

The vast majority (96%) of those interviewed in Italy who had crossed to Europe via the Central Mediterranean route took a boat from Libya. However, their journeys to reach Libya originated in a wide range of different locations and were extremely varied. Respondents from the countries of West Africa (Benin, Burkina Faso, Cameroon, Gambia, Ghana, Guinea, Ivory Coast, Mali, Nigeria, Senegal, Sierra Leone and Togo) often set out originally to local and regional destinations in buses, cars and lorries on journeys organised at short notice by travel agencies, friends or family members. This enabled people to get away quickly from situations of violence or personal danger (McMahon and Sigona, 2016). People from East Africa (Eritrea, Ethiopia, Somalia and Sudan), often moved first to relatively nearby destinations, perhaps to a refugee camp in Sudan. Others moved further afield, often to Khartoum in the first instance. Particularly in the case of Eritrea, where snipers are reportedly ordered to shoot those seeking to leave the country, this involved crossing dangerous borders on foot. People subsequently moved on towards Libya, and to a lesser extent Egypt or Algeria.

We identified four principal routes which converged in Libya and fed into the Central Mediterranean crossing:

- *a North African route* originating in Morocco, Tunisia, Libya or Egypt;
- *a West African route* originating in countries of West and Central Africa, made up of highly fragmented and often lengthy trajectories with multiple stops along the way, converging in Burkina Faso, Mali and then Niger on the way to Libya;
- *an East African route* originating in the Horn of Africa, made up of fragmented and long trajectories with various stops, and onwards by air to Turkey or overland to Libya or Egypt;
- *routes from the rest of the world* originating in countries beyond Africa such as Syria (air travel to Egypt, overland to Libya), Pakistan and Bangladesh (air travel to Libya). These routes converged with the others in Libya.

The convergence of these different routes to form the Eastern and Central Mediterranean routes into Europe via Turkey and Greece can be clearly seen in Figure 3.3.

Duration of migration

There was significant variation in the time taken from the point at which people left their home country or the country in which they were living to the point at which they arrived in Europe. Whereas some reached Europe in a matter of days, others had departed from their country of origin years, even decades, before arriving at the place where we met them. We identified three overall patterns.

First, the average duration of migration for those arriving in Greece via the Eastern Mediterranean route was considerably shorter than that found for those arriving via the Central Mediterranean route to Italy or Malta (Figure 3.4). Indeed, nearly two-thirds (61%) of those who were interviewed in Greece arrived within six months of departure from their country of origin, compared with only 32% of those who were interviewed in Italy and Malta. And while a third of people arrived in Greece within one month, just 1% of respondents who travelled through Africa arrived in Italy and Malta so quickly. Rapid journeys into Greece were most common among respondents from Iraq, the majority of whom (86%) arrived in less than one month, and Syria, almost half (44%) of whom arrived in Greece less than one month after leaving their home (Figure 3.5).

Second, for those arriving via the Central Mediterranean route it was more likely that several months had passed since they had departed from their place of origin compared with those travelling via the Eastern Mediterranean route. Only 15% of those travelling across the Eastern Mediterranean route had been travelling for 7–18 months compared with one-third (34%) of those arriving in Italy. In fact, among respondents travelling through the Central Mediterranean route, only those from the Maghreb countries were able to travel quickly. For most respondents, migration to Europe was the culmination of a much lengthier process involving both short and/

Figure 3.3: Convergence of routes through the Eastern and Central Mediterranean (122 respondents)

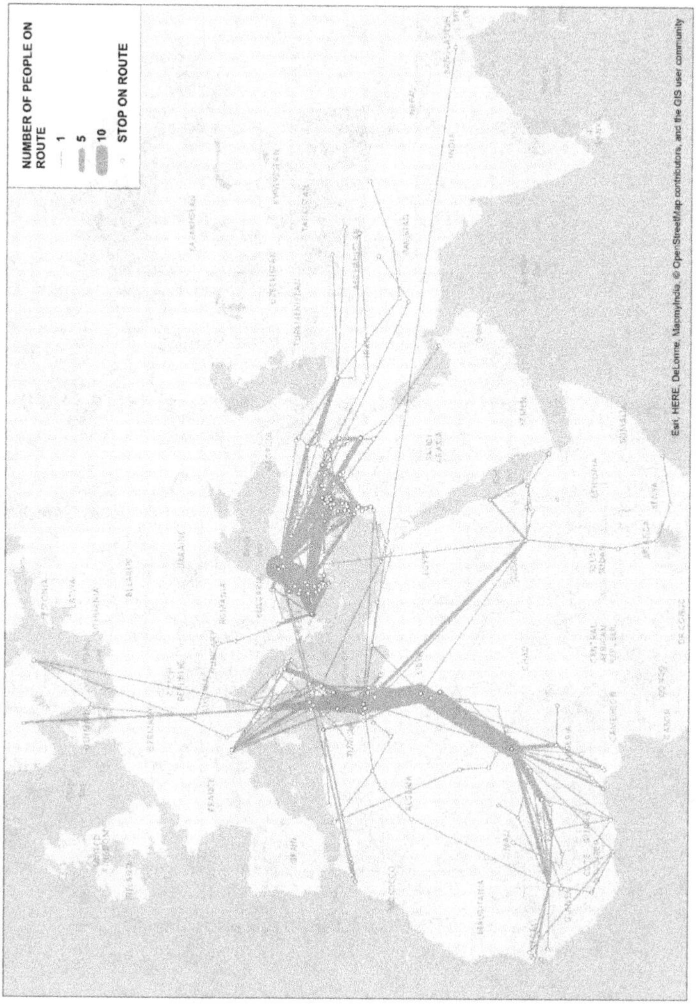

Figure 3.4: Duration of migration by country of arrival through the Eastern Mediterranean route to Greece and Central Mediterranean route to Italy and Malta (in months)

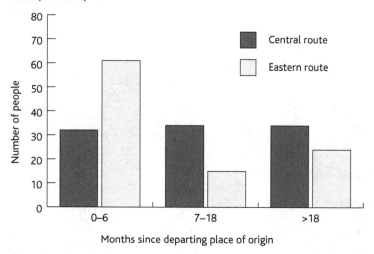

Months since departing place of origin

Figure 3.5: Duration of migration for Syrian and Iraqi nationals to Greece (in months)

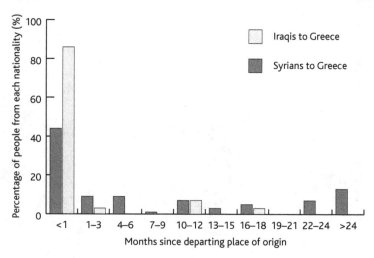

Months since departing place of origin

or long stops in various locations. This was particularly the case for people originating in West African countries, who had often stopped in countries within the region and in Libya prior to moving onward across the sea (Figure 3.6). People who had been in Libya spent, on average, seven months there.

Third, many of those travelling along both routes left their country of origin years before arriving in Europe. Nearly a quarter (24%) of those who travelled the Eastern Mediterranean route and one-third (34%) who travelled along the Central Mediterranean route had left their countries of origin more than 18 months previously.[2] This pattern featured particularly strongly among Afghans who arrived in Greece, often after residing in Iran where the average length of a stay was three and a half years. Similarly, for Eritreans the time between departure from the home country and arrival in Europe was particularly lengthy as some had stayed for extended periods in Sudan, Egypt or Israel (Figure 3.7).

Figure 3.6: Duration of migration for nationals from West African countries (in months)

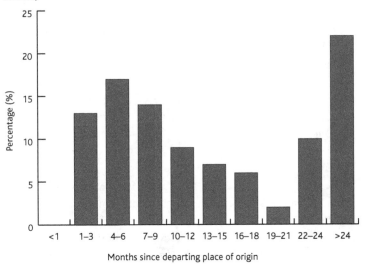

Months since departing place of origin

Figure 3.7: Duration of migration for Eritrean and Afghan nationals to Greece and Italy combined (in months)

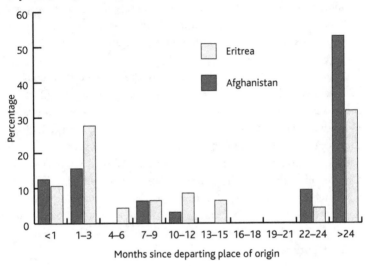

This overview shows the diverse geography of routes and timescales for migration of those arriving in Europe in 2015. At the same time, it also highlights patterns of convergence into more or less discernible routes leading towards the countries of southern Europe. The question, however, is how and why these diverse migration flows came together in the way that they did. In order to explain this, we need to take a closer look at how these movements developed over time.

Unpacking migration patterns

The previous section set out the geography of the journeys that made up the different routes to and across the Mediterranean Sea. In this section we will look at these varied movements in more detail, focusing in particular on when and why people stopped or had their journeys interrupted, and when and why they then continued moving on. The way that these journeys and stops fit together is central to our understanding of the nature of the migration patterns to and across the Mediterranean. Drawing on our data we can identify three distinct types of migration characterised by varying patterns of migration and stops:

- one-off migration between two places, usually through relatively direct and fast *journeys*, which may be interspersed only by short stops;
- longer *migration trajectories* of separate journeys linked together, interrupted by longer stops in one or more countries;
- *serial migration* of consecutive movements, separated by periods of significant duration spent in one or more different locations, from which onward movement can be considered a separate migration experience driven by its own motivations, decision-making, planning and aspirations.

It is important to note that these three types of migration are not always easily differentiated. For example, many individuals did not consider themselves to be on a 'migration trajectory' at the outset, but made decisions to move on in response to the particular situation in which they had found themselves. We explore the reasons why they decided to move on in Chapter Six. Others may have intended to move quickly between two places but found that it was impossible to do so or, alternatively, had chosen to stay in a place due to their own shifting personal or family circumstances. Nonetheless, understanding these different types of movement is important and necessary in order to better understand the dynamics of migration in the Mediterranean region and, in particular, to unpack the ways in which these dynamics shaped the arrival of people to Europe via the Central and Eastern Mediterranean routes.

The nature of stops and stays

Focusing on the nature of stops and stays helps us to explore the difference between more or less unified and direct journeys to Europe and longer-term, often fragmented trajectories and serial migration decisions. While people often made multiple stops in different countries before arriving in Europe, the number of stops made in different countries varied significantly. Respondents made, on average, three or four stops within Turkey, for example, while in Libya the average was only two.

In most cases, the initial journeys from countries of origin were directed towards nearby locations. Many Syrians often made a first stop within Syria, becoming internally displaced before subsequently moving across an international border.

> I was living in Raqqa. We went by car to another area in Raqqa which was controlled by the regime…[then] we went to Palmyra, and from there to Damascus [then] we went by coach to the border with Lebanon. (Syrian man travelling with his wife and three children aged 11, 7 and 4 years old and a baby aged 8 months)

West and East African respondents commonly moved initially to nearby towns or cities. For example, Gambian respondents often stopped in Casamance on the border with Senegal while Eritreans sometimes made their first stop in a refugee camp near the border between Eritrea and Ethiopia or Sudan.

> I spent one year and two months in the Adi-Harush refugee camp, it was organised by UNHCR, there were multiple people, many many people there…life was bad, there was a shortage of food, no communication and I had no communication with my family or the world outside. So I left the camp to go to Sudan. (Eritrean man aged 36)

It is clear from our research that stops and stays are of a qualitatively different nature and that they can have various potential functions for those on the move. They can be intended or unintended, voluntary or forced. Some of those we spoke to described decisions to stop in a town or city in order to rest, settle, work, gather resources or connect with onward transport. These stops were short in duration. Indeed, certain countries such as Niger were more clearly places where people had only ever intended to stop for a short time. Others can be defined as involuntary stops or stays due to violence and conflict, experiences of crime, a lack of money, arrest or kidnappings, detention or poor health. These kinds of stops were more commonly reported on the borders of Chad and Sudan as well as in Libya (see Chapter Six).

The story of Arash, a 50-year-old Afghan man travelling with his wife and five teenage children illustrates how the journey can sometimes be very quick even when it involves a large number of stops (Box 3.3). His journey from Kabul to Athens took just two weeks, yet by the time we interviewed Arash in Greece, the family had already completed ten separate legs of their journey and had crossed five countries. This type of overland journey was typical among those who were unable to access visas to travel legally. Although the destination was clear from the outset, arrangements for travel were made as the journey unfolded.

Box 3.3: From Kabul to Athens in two weeks: the story of Arash

I worked for a German company. I have received many death threats. I was forced to leave Afghanistan. Some of my relatives left Afghanistan earlier than me and have meanwhile arrived in Germany. I want to go to Germany or anywhere they can give me asylum. In Kabul, you can't get a passport and can't apply for a visa. From Kabul, we went to Buldak [Afghanistan] by bus, close to the border with Pakistan. From there we crossed illegally to Baluchistan [Pakistan], we walked a lot there. From there we went to the border with Iran and we crossed to Kerman [Iran]. Then we went to Shiraz. From Kabul to Shiraz it took us six days. I paid US$3,000 for the whole family, food and smuggling fees included. From Shiraz, we went to Tehran where we found a smuggler to Turkey. The smugglers that brought us to Shiraz gave us the phone number of the smuggler in Tehran. We made a deal with him to send us to Istanbul for US$900 per person. After three days we arrived in Istanbul and we stayed for one day in a square there. In that square, we found a guy who was speaking both Turkish and Farsi and told him that we want to go to Germany. We made a deal with him to send us to Greece for €800 per person. We left the same day from Istanbul to the coast by bus. The bus went inside a ferry at some point, and after that we arrived at the coast. The boat was an inflatable. When we arrived, there were already many people on the beach waiting for us. A bus on the island took us from the beach to the camp. We stayed for one day on that island, we stayed for one day at the camp, and we were registered there. Now, we are staying in this square [Victoria square in Athens]. I will try to find some money to continue the journey to Germany. I know that the bus ticket to the FYROM border costs €30. I have no idea how the situation is after the Greek–FYROM border.

Others stops, by contrast, were of medium or extended duration and reflected an intention on the part of an individual to live in that particular location. They can thus be characterised as a 'stay' rather than just a 'stop'. Those who had decided to stay usually had no initial intention of moving on, whereas those who had stopped temporarily viewed this as punctuating a broader migration trajectory which had a distinct location as its intended destination.

Serial migration and longer-term trajectories

For some people the migration experience was, as we have noted, relatively short and direct. However, this was certainly not the case for everyone. For around a quarter of all of our respondents it is clear that the countries to which they had originally travelled – including Iran, Sudan and Libya – were initially perceived as destination countries where they intended to settle and live. This conclusion is supported by the fact that over 2.5 million refugees continue to live in Turkey and over 980,000 in Iran (UNHCR, 2016). Often, during these longer periods of stay people worked, ran a business, rented accommodation or even applied for immigration status. People often experienced some degree of integration into local social systems. In many cases they did not intend to move on until there was a particular change in their circumstances. As a result, their onward migration can be considered a separate migration experience driven by its own motivations, decision-making, planning and aspirations.

The experiences of Amadou, a young single Gambian man who left his home country due to family problems associated with religious tensions, are illustrative of these types of journeys to Europe. They involve longer periods of stay in an effort to find work and an opportunity to rebuild a life (Box 3.4). Amadou did not plan his journey or prepare for his migration, nor did he intend to come to Europe when he first left Gambia. Instead, he was propelled forward by conditions in one place or attracted by promises of opportunities in another. His entire migration trajectory was the result of a chain of incidents and chance encounters rather than being pre-planned. He spent time in four countries before arriving in Italy, often working to support himself. Other people – 'a man', 'a friend', 'an old man' – who encouraged him to move on were crucial to the migration trajectory that developed. Meanwhile certain locations, notably 'garages' (meaning central bus stations), provided important places for connecting with other people who might be able to provide opportunities. The importance of these locations was also mentioned by many other people we spoke to.

Box 3.4: From Gambia to Turin in 22 months: the story of Amadou

Amadou, a young Gambian man in his mid-twenties, left his home town and country because of family problems related to religious tensions. He left home in a rush and first hid in a friend's house but soon afterwards, in January 2014, he left Gambia. Amadou travelled first by bus to Senegal but he didn't feel safe: 'it was the same like staying in Gambia'. Instead he decided to move to neighbouring Mali, staying in the capital, Bamako, for two months. At the 'garage' (central bus station) he met an old man who helped him to get odd jobs. The old man had another friend, a bus driver. One day the bus driver suggested that Amadou accompany him to find a job in Agadez in Niger. Once in Agadez, Amadou realised that Bamako was actually better in terms of job opportunities and general living conditions but could not go back because he had no money. Instead he stayed in another 'garage' where he made friends with a man who found him work as a bricklayer. Amadou stayed in Agadez for three months but 'the man told me that if I go to Libya, I will find a good job'. Amadou knew nothing about the security situation and decided to go to Libya because 'in Niger there was nothing'. The journey to Qatrun in Libya took four days. There, he met a compatriot who worked as auto-body repairer and within a few days was recruited by the same garage. The job was good, he was regularly paid and ended up staying in Qatrun for two or three months. At some point, his Gambian friend told him that he wanted to go to Tripoli because he believed that he would find a better job there. Amadou decided to go with him and found a job after just a few weeks but he felt unsafe. One day he was stopped by the police. Because he didn't have any ID papers, Amadou was imprisoned for three months before he was able to escape. An old man offered to him lodgings in return for assistance with household chores. He lived there for four months but was then told to leave. The man had a friend who took Amadou to Zuwara on the coast. From there Amadou travelled to Italy, eventually arriving in Taranto from where he was transferred to Turin. He arrived in Turin 22 months after leaving Gambia.

Eritreans were involved in perhaps the most complex migration processes and journeys, often including stays of over a year in countries including Sudan, Egypt, Israel and Uganda. The decision to move on was often made only when economic opportunities appeared to have run out, when corruption was seen as too much of an obstacle or when new situations of insecurity arose. For example, we spoke with Syrians who had intended to stay permanently in Egypt until the government of Abdeh Fattah el-Sisi brought in increasing restrictions and repression of everyday life.

> I'm originally from Daraa. I left in December 2012. We decided to go to Egypt. We took a plane from Amman to Alexandria. President Morsi was still there and Syrians could enter by plane. They were welcome in Egypt. I lived there about a year and a half...I worked as a transporter of goods by truck...When the Morsi government fell and Al Sisi arrived things for Syrians changed. Strong discrimination. Even renewing a residence permit was difficult. So I went to Libya...Libya is terrible...I set aside money to leave and I took the boat to Italy. (Syrian man aged 23)

We also spoke with Palestinian refugees who had resided for many years, or been born, in Syria before being displaced by the conflict. Similarly, many respondents from West African countries and from Bangladesh had intended to stay in Libya for work, but no longer felt safe there (see Chapter Six).

Of all the countries which respondents passed through, stopped and stayed in, it was Iran where people spent the longest amount of time, an average of three and a half years. Indeed, a quarter (27%) of those who had been living in Iran had stayed there for longer than this, for between 10 to 40 years. These were all Afghans who had left Afghanistan due to conflict and who lived in Iran. For these refugees and migrants, the decision to travel to Europe should be understood as part of a broader pattern of serial migration and multiple, sometimes entirely unrelated, decisions to migrate. We explore the experiences of our Afghan respondents in more detail in Chapter Six. The complex nature of these longer-term migration trajectories challenges the idea that refugees and migrants were heading for Europe in 2015 and requires us to look much more closely and carefully at the reasons why they decided to leave, where they wanted to go and how they ended up being in Europe. These experiences form the basis of the analysis in the chapters that follow.

Notes

[1] See www.iom.int/news/iom-records-over-60000-migrants-passing-through-agadez-niger-between-february-and-april-2016
[2] These numbers do not add to 100% due to a lack of complete information on duration of journeys for some of our interviewees.

FOUR

The decision to leave

We don't know who is to blame for what is happening in Syria but the Syrian people pay the price. We had our jobs, we had our businesses. Then one day we lost everything. We can find no peace in Syria. I was afraid that the regime will force my sons to join the army. (Syrian woman aged 47 travelling with her 21-year-old son)

Having unpacked the routes taken by refugees and migrants in the previous chapter, we now turn our attention to the reasons why people decided to leave their home countries, focusing in particular on the role of conflict, persecution and human rights abuse, but also unpacking the complex and often overlapping relationship between 'forced' and 'economic' drivers of migration. This is important, in part to give voice to the diverse stories of individuals and families who ended up risking their lives to cross the Mediterranean, but also because their stories challenge the assumptions underpinning Europe's policy response (discussed further in Chapter Eight).

Conflict, persecution and human rights abuse

According to IOM (2016a), nearly 82% of those arriving in Greece and Italy in 2015 originated from just four countries: Syria, Afghanistan, Iraq and Eritrea. These are countries which were experiencing protracted political unrest and conflict and which have well-documented records of human rights abuse (EASO, 2016b; Amnesty International, 2017a; HRW, 2017). While the factors driving migration are complex and vary among those travelling to Europe via the Eastern and Central Mediterranean routes, our research confirms the conclusions of HRW (2015), IOM (2016c), and others (for example, Squire et al, 2017), that conflict, insecurity and human rights abuse in the countries neighbouring Europe – most notably the war in Syria – were the main factors driving people from their homes and towards Europe in 2015.

When we asked our respondents to describe the circumstances under which they had decided to leave, more than three-quarters (77%) of respondents across the entire sample (both Central and Eastern Mediterranean routes) explicitly mentioned factors that could be described as 'forced migration', including conflict, persecution, violence, death threats and human rights abuse. The figure was even higher (91%) for those interviewed in Greece, reflecting the significant proportion of people moving from situations of conflict in Syria, Iraq and Afghanistan who travelled across the Aegean from Turkey.

Generalised violence and insecurity

Many of those we spoke to in Greece had not been specifically targeted but had left their countries because levels of violence and insecurity had become intolerable. They had consequently feared for their own personal safety and that of their families. Syrians who were living in areas of conflict in Syria and who were subject to almost daily barrel bombings, sniper fire and other attacks were especially fearful. Homs, Damascus and Aleppo were frequently mentioned as cities in which it had become impossible to live.

I was living in Damascus. The situation was bad. I was working as a civil servant for 16 years. We were renting, expensive rent. The schools closed down. The regime was dropping bombs every day. There was no future there. I decided to leave one year ago from Syria for my children. Everybody leaves Syria for the sake of their children. (Syrian man aged 35 travelling to Germany to join his wife and four children)

The experiences of a 36-year-old Syrian man travelling with his wife and two young children aged 5 and 2 years reflects the desperation and fear of many of those with whom we spoke (Box 4.1).

Box 4.1: 'Every day we were dying and born again': the ongoing conflict in Syria

I was living in Al-Zabadani, Syria. There is not even one house left standing there. Every two minutes you might die. The city does not exist anymore. IS and the regime are collaborating, they are fighting together against the Free Syrian Army (FSA). We have gone to Damascus for a short trip two years ago. Neighbours called us from Al-Zabadani and told us that our house had been bombed. We went to live in a village, Al-Buwaidah al-Sharqiyah. I found a job there, I was selling clothes. We rented a house. My wife was bringing the clothes herself from Damascus and I was selling them in that shop. It was very dangerous what my wife was doing. It's not allowed to go back and forth between cities. The regime was kidnapping people and asking for ransom. They were killing people. Whatever you do there, you can find no peace. Every day we were dying and born again. Two months ago, I decided to leave. It was like taking a decision to commit suicide. I wanted to get away from both the regime and the FSA. I was looking for a way to avoid both. I did it for my children. They have been psychologically traumatised because of the war.

Iraqi respondents described at length, and in great detail, the consequences of the escalating conflict, particularly in cities such as Baghdad and Mosul where life had become very difficult for many. As in Syria, there was a constant fear of death, reinforced by experiences of violence, personal injury and the deaths of friends and relatives.

I was living in Baghdad. You don't know when you are going to die there. (Iraqi man aged 28 travelling with his wife and 4-year-old son)

Those from Sunni backgrounds told us that they felt particularly vulnerable:

I was living in Nasiriyah. I was a driver. I was working for pennies. And it was hard even to find such a job paying pennies. The government sent me a letter which said that I had to join the army. They sent me the letter twice. I received the last one 10 days ago. It said that I had to join the army in 30 days. I am Sunni, and the government can harm me any time. Being Sunni is enough to harm you. The government can put you in prison or it can kill you. (Iraqi man aged 38)

Respondents from Syria and Iraq described kidnapping by state and non-state agencies (including a range of militia groups) as an increasingly frequent threat to their safety and that of their families. In some cases, individuals were targeted because they were perceived to be a threat. More commonly however it was because they had resources and it was thought that their families would pay a significant ransom for their return.

Most probably, it's the regime which conducts the kidnaps but you can never be sure. In 2013, regime soldiers came to my house and kidnapped me. I spent two months in prison. I was being beaten up every day [Respondent shows the interviewer burn marks from cigarettes on his body]. I spent 25 days in the hospital. I later learned that the regime had written in their report that I was involved with the FSA. (Syrian man aged 56 travelling with his 27-year-old son)

Towards the end of the fieldwork phase (January 2016) we also met a growing number of Yemenis who had moved due to escalating bombing raids on civilian areas by Saudi Arabia (HRW, 2016a). All were young men aged between 18 and 25 years who came from relatively wealthy families who had been able to sell some of their possessions, most notably jewellery, to fund their sons' exit from the country. Most of these young men were in education or employment. Almost all said that they and their families were concerned that they would be forcibly recruited into the Al-Houthi rebel forces.

> My family and I used to have a good life, before the war started again in Yemen. My family decided to get me out of the country because of the Al-Houthi, who forcibly recruits young men. There are few safe places in Yemen now, and not for long. Bombs explode every day. A bomb killed my cousin. That's when my family decided to send me abroad. The next day, they sent my passport to Saudi Arabia to get me a visa. They were telling me, 'You have talent, it is better for you to flee abroad.' (Yemeni man aged 19)

While the composition of people travelling to Europe via the Central Mediterranean route was more diverse (see Chapter Two), nearly two-thirds (66%) of those who were interviewed in Italy and Malta made reference to factors associated with 'forced migration' when telling us why they decided to leave their home countries. Many more had experienced conflict, persecution and human rights abuses in the countries to which they subsequently moved, most notably Libya. This finding is in line with that of IOM (2016c), which found that economic or work reasons were the main reasons for migration among only 24% of the 1,031 refugees and migrants whom they interviewed.

In Italy, as in Greece, we met people who described having to leave because of escalating tensions and conflict: between Muslims and Christians in some countries (most notably some areas of Nigeria); intergenerational conflicts related to family and marriage (including familial conflicts arising from an individual's choice of partner); religious obligations which sometimes manifested themselves as violent rituals together with land disputes; and fights among extended families. Tensions around religious and fraternity affiliations leading to physical violence and even the murder of close family members were recurrent themes in our interviews with Nigerian men in particular. While these conflicts may be localised or regional – and therefore not well understood by the international community – they represent a significant threat to the lives of those affected.

Beyond these general experiences of conflict and violence, three particular issues affected a significant proportion of those interviewed in all of our case study countries: persecution arising from actual or assumed political activities/opposition; the impact of IS and other armed militias; and indefinite forced conscription.

Political activism and engagement

I decided to leave because I was left alone with my children. My husband was in prison and later killed. He was a journalist in Eritrea…several letters had arrived about joining the military service which he had so far managed to escape with false medical certificates. He was arrested and tortured. They wanted information on opponents that he did not have. And they killed him. (Eritrean woman aged 35)

Although many of those we spoke to were fleeing generalised conflict and violence that was not specific to them, others had been singled out for harm either because of their ethnic or religious identity (as with the Sunni in Iraq) or because of their political activism and engagement in various forms of resistance. Among those interviewed in Greece these included: a member of the opposition Pakistan People's Party in Pakistan; a Syrian who was arrested and imprisoned because the authorities thought that he would participate in a political protest; a Syrian MP who opposed the actions of the Assad regime; a Syrian Airforce Colonel who was tortured for refusing to drop barrel bombs; and a Syrian former solider in Assad's army who left and became a founder of the FSA. Respondents who had been journalists, humanitarian and CSO workers and activists were also targeted in Syria and Iraq.

Box 4.2: Targeting of political opposition in Syria: Amed's story

Amed was living in Damascus where he was studying to become a doctor. He explained that in order to become a doctor or a lawyer in Syria it was necessary to support the Ba'ath party, the ruling party of Bashar al-Assad, the President of Syria: 'You need to be a member of the Assad's party. They give you a card and a phone number, which you have to call in case you hear somebody saying bad things about the party. I denied becoming a member of that party.' Amed had experienced difficulties from the age of 16 years when he started his military service and was sent letters asking him to explain why he had not joined the party: 'They wanted to know everything about me. They forced me to repeat an academic year during my university studies due to my political beliefs. They warned me that this would happen all my life if I didn't join Assad's party.' Amed left Syria and travelled to Saudi Arabia to join his father in April 2011, 20 days after the revolution started but he decided to return in order to document what was happening: 'I was watching on TV that the situation in Syria was deteriorating. However, I returned to Syria two months later. It wasn't easy for me to sit and observe the regime killing people. I returned in order to help people there. I went to Damascus, Aleppo and Homs. I started taking photos and recording videos of the regime's atrocities. I wanted to send these photos to news channels.' Amed moved from city to city but in late 2011 was attacked and taken into detention where he was interrogated about the photographs he had taken, beaten and tortured. Ahmed was released unexpectedly because the head of the prison knew his father. He went to live with his mother helping people who had been displaced within Syria: 'I was a one-man NGO for one year. I was giving them medicines, clothes, whatever I had. I was approached many times to fight with the regime. But I denied taking a gun and killing people. I was receiving threats for a year.' He was about to get married but his wife-to-be and her family were killed when a bomb hit their house just five days before the ceremony. In December 2012 Amed decided to go to Lebanon where his brother was living. He stayed there for nearly a year but found it impossible to secure work so he and the remaining members of his family went to Jordan before travelling on to Turkey and Greece.

A number of those travelling through the Central Mediterranean route had also decided to leave their homes due to political persecution or localised situations of civil unrest. Respondents from places as diverse as Gambia, Nigeria and Pakistan spoke of violence due to their membership of a political party, the threat of imprisonment and facing corrupt or unfair legal processes. Nearly a third (29%) of the Nigerian women we spoke to told us that that they were politically active or that the murder of a close, usually male, family member – husband, brother, father – had destabilised both their personal security and their livelihood. This combination of political and economic factors underpinned the decision to leave.

> I'm an activist. I had a problem with the government because I speak out, I speak for the people. My husband was murdered and I was in danger. (Nigerian woman aged 37)

The threat posed by armed groups

More than a quarter (28%) of respondents interviewed in Greece said that a significant factor in their decision to leave was the activities of IS, particularly in Syria but also in Iraq, Afghanistan and Yemen. These respondents had been detained, tortured or forced to watch beheadings. They expressed grave concerns for the safety of their families, and particularly women (wives, sisters, daughters) who were perceived to be non-compliant with strict Sharia laws concerning their dress and behaviour.

> I was living in Raqqa. Raqqa equals Daesh! There was nothing good there. There was no freedom. You couldn't even walk in the streets freely. Your wife has to be covered from head to toes…You could die at any moment by IS or the regime. I am a devout Muslim. I was praying five times a day but since IS came I lost my enthusiasm for praying. (Syrian man aged 32 travelling with his wife and four children aged 11, 7, 4 years and 8 months)

While the activities of IS were not prevalent in the accounts of those travelling through the Central Mediterranean route, respondents whose journeys originated in West Africa described the dangers posed by armed groups such as the Movement of Democratic Forces of Casamance in Senegal, terrorist organisations including Boko Haram and particular confraternities, such as Black Axe in Nigeria. A number of people also described violence at the hands of terrorist groups including Al-Shabaab in Somalia (Box 4.3). While some of these people also spoke about poverty, their inability to make a living was almost invariably situated within a broader context of political insecurity and fears of being forcibly conscripted. One young man told us that he had fled Somalia when his father was killed by Al-Shabaab as a result of his work for the Somalian Information Office, others that they would be forced to join Al-Shabaab:

I decided to leave Somalia because there is no hope of a good future there. Al-Shabaab was active about 10km from where we lived. My father was a soldier for the old government so Al-Shabaab killed him. Then Al-Shabaab came to me and tried to recruit me to fight for them but I refused. When I rejected their invite, they claimed that I was against Islam and they arrested me and put me in a prison and threatened to kill me. I had to escape. In the middle of the night, the Somali government attacked the prison that I was being held in and I saw my chance to escape. Al-Shabaab couldn't fight me while they were fighting the government so I was able to get away. (Somali man aged 21)

Box 4.3: Al-Shabaab in Somalia

Somalia remained the third largest country of origin for refugees during 2015 with the number of refugees increasing marginally from 1.11 million to 1.12 million (UNHCR 2016). As with all other refugee populations, the majority of Somali refugees were hosted in neighbouring countries: Kenya and Ethiopia continue to host large numbers of refugees originating from Somalia, with 417,900 and 256,700 Somali refugees at the end of 2015, respectively. Other countries hosting large numbers of Somalis included Yemen (253,200), South Africa (41,500), and Uganda (27,700). There were 21,285 applications for asylum in the 28 EU Member States during the course of 2015 (EASO, 2016b).

According to HRW (2017), civilians in Somalia continue to report abuses by a number of different factions as well as dire humanitarian conditions. Many of these problems are associated with Al-Shabaab – meaning 'The Youth' in Arabic – which is the largest militant organisation fighting to oust the Somali government.[1] The group seeks to control territory within Somalia in order to establish a society based on its rigid interpretation of Sharia law. Targeted attacks by Al-Shabaab on civilians and civilian infrastructure with suicide bombings and improvised explosive devices (IEDs) have had devastating effects, killing, maiming and displacing large numbers of people. More than 50,000 civilians were killed, injured or displaced as a result of the armed conflict and generalised violence during 2015 (Amnesty International, 2017b). All parties to the conflict were responsible for violations of human rights and international humanitarian law, some amounting to war crimes. In addition, the population living under Al-Shabaab's harsh interpretation of Sharia law experience severe restrictions to their freedom of movement, expression and association (EASO, 2016b; Amnesty International, 2017b).

Forced conscription

Concerns about being forcibly recruited into the army or other military groups were a recurrent theme in interviews with respondents from a number of countries from which our respondents originated. These countries included Iraq, where there has been a protracted conflict beginning with the 2003 invasion by a US-led coalition, and which has more recently seen intensified conflict with IS. Several Afghans also told us that they had been conscripted into the Iranian army to support the Assad regime in Syria, including a 16-year-old child whose mother told us what had happened to her son.[2] However, it was among Eritreans that we heard most about the effects of forced conscription.

While migration within and out of the Horn of Africa is not a new phenomenon, the scale of recent movements has been dramatic. In a region with an estimated 242 million inhabitants, the Horn of Africa hosts over 8.7 million displaced persons, including over 6.5 million internally displaced persons (IDPs) and about 2.2 million refugees (UNHCR and World Bank, 2015). An estimated 5,000 Eritreans leave the country each month, making it one of the world's top producers of refugees (ODI, 2017). Eritreans decide to leave for various reasons, but the main drivers are endemic poverty, a lack of livelihood opportunities, and limited political freedoms (UNHCR, 2011; Horwood and Hooper, 2016; Campbell, 2017). A UN inquiry in 2015 found that the Eritrean government was responsible for systematic, widespread and gross human rights violations. It has created a climate of fear in which dissent is stifled and a large proportion of the population is subjected to forced labour and imprisonment (OHCHR, 2015). In recent years an estimated 400,000 people (nearly 10% of the population) have left the country, mainly young men of military conscription age (ODI, 2017). Compulsory military service for all has been described by refugees and observers as oppressive and potentially unlimited in length (Campbell, 2017; MSF, 2017; ODI, 2017).

Reflecting this, virtually all of our Eritrean respondents described 'endless military service' as the principal driver of their decision to leave. For many people the issue of forced military conscription was combined with a lack of opportunities to earn a decent salary, see or spend time with their family or continue with their chosen educational path. We opened this book with the story of Michael and Niyat who left Eritrea because they could no longer tolerate a life of forced conscription which made it impossible for them to be together or live a normal life. Michael had been conscripted into the army at a young age. After 14 years of being forced to work for virtually nothing, and with no release date in sight, Michael decided he could take no more. His wife Niyat told us:

> In Eritrea, national military service is required and there is no end date so you never know when you will get out of the military. I don't agree with this policy and we don't want to be forced to fight. My husband and I decided to leave Eritrea because we didn't want a life of compulsory military service.

Their comments were echoed by others.

> I was working as a teacher in Ashmara. I was also working as an artist. I decided to leave because I was imprisoned more than once by the government. I was imprisoned for the first

time when I was in college and for the second time, after my graduation…After I graduated and even though I had already started working as a teacher, they wanted to send me to SAWA.[3] I told them I can't go and they sent me to prison again for four months. It is an underground prison. I was living with almost 1,000 people. That was when I decided to leave this country. (Eritrean man aged 34)

Poverty and economic factors

Although the majority of those we spoke to described, often in great detail, how conflict, persecution and human rights abuse had been key factors in their decision to leave, many also told us that their decision was motivated by economic factors and the need to find work to support themselves and their families. The circumstances varied: some people wanted to get a job that would enable them to move beyond a hand-to-mouth existence; others wanted to gain experience so that they could improve their prospects in their home countries; others wanted to be able to send remittances from abroad to their families back home. At times, both security and economic factors were mentioned by our respondents. While poverty and economic factors often appear to be, and sometimes are, the primary motivation for the decision to leave, these factors often overlap with political factors in complex ways.

[He] comes from a poor family…His eldest brother was the only one with a regular job and he provided for the family: he was a 'big politician' but he has been killed by members of the rival party…[he] decided to emigrate in order to find a job and maintain his family. At that time the only possibility was to go to Libya, as there he could obtain a visa. (Bangladeshi man aged 18)

Violence, political persecution or corruption can not only put an individual's life in danger, but also harms their capacity to provide for themselves and their family. People from West African countries including Gambia and Côte d'Ivoire, for example, spoke of crime, political corruption and violence as factors which undermined economic opportunities both in their country and for them personally. People from Bangladesh told us that they moved to Libya with labour agencies only to find themselves with enormous debts or at risk of being forced to work for nothing. An Ethiopian man moved initially to live in a refugee camp after his father was unjustly imprisoned, but continued moving further away to find opportunities which would enable him to support his family. Such examples highlight the ways that security, political, economic and personal reasons for leaving places often impact on one another.

In countries where there has been protracted conflict, people were not only fearful for their safety but also found it impossible to feed themselves and their families. The war had undermined the ability to earn a livelihood by killing primary breadwinners, destroying businesses and making it impossible to travel to work. This was seen most clearly in Syria, where the conflict has devastated the economic infrastructure of the country and the wider Levant region, increasing the prices of basic goods and commodities including food and oil (Ianchovichina and Ivanic, 2014; Gobat and Kostial, 2016). Price increases have been exacerbated by internal displacement and the movement of large numbers of people to some of the safer cities.

> People started flowing into Afrin from across Syria because there was peace...The cost of living increased incredibly. Afrin is a very expensive city now. (Syrian man aged 33)

This evidence from across the two routes suggests that there is often a complex and overlapping relationship between 'forced' and 'economic' drivers of migration to Europe. Many respondents told us that they had taken the decision to move for economic reasons but it was conflict that had created their economic insecurity. Equally many of those who had initially moved for primarily economic reasons to countries such as Libya, then found themselves facing violence and insecurity. We explore these issues further in Chapter Six.

Deciding where to go

Deciding to leave and where to go is rarely an easy. The people we spoke to did everything they could to mitigate the risks. This included travelling together in family groups, with friends – some of whom they met *en route* – and gathering all the money they could prior to departure through borrowing and selling possessions. For many, being able to gather sufficient money was not just an important strategy for mitigating risk, but a precondition for leaving. People knew their journeys would be expensive, with significant amounts of money needed to pay smugglers, living expenses, bribes and for transportation where this was not arranged through smugglers (see Chapter Five). A significant proportion of respondents had borrowed the money from relatives, with families often invested in the decision of the individual to travel. Difficult decisions had to be made about who could, and could not, leave given the risks of the journeys and resource constraints.

> It was very hard to gather the money for the journey. I sold our furniture, my wife's jewellery and my land in order to come here. And I was also saving money. We left Aleppo with my wife and children and went to Afrin where our family house was. I tried to work there but the money I was earning was not enough. My wife suggested me to go to Turkey. (Syrian man aged 33 who had to leave his wife and children aged 6 and 4 behind in Syria)

There is a widely held view expressed by European politicians and some sections of the media that refugees and migrants have a sufficiently detailed knowledge about migration policy in the countries of Europe to be able make rational and informed choices about their intended destinations. The impression given is that the vast majority of refugees and migrants in Africa and the Middle East are on their way to Europe, 'pulled' by the prospect of securing jobs and access to welfare support. There is also a perception that increased arrivals in 2015 were caused largely by the German Chancellor Angela Merkel's statement at the end of August that *'wir schaffen das'* ('we can do it') in response to increased numbers arriving from Syria and elsewhere, and her decision on 5 September to accept thousands of refugees who had set out to walk from Keleti Station in Budapest to Germany.

Our research, like that of other studies exploring this issue in the context of recent arrivals in Europe (see for example, Hagen-Zanker and Mallett, 2016; IOM, 2016c, Squire et al, 2017), found that when refugees and migrants initially set out from their place of origin they often did not have very clear plans about where their final destination would be. This was the case for the majority of those we spoke to. Michael and Niyat, the Eritrean couple who we met in the introduction to this book, told us that initially they had not intended to come to Europe.

> I didn't plan to go to Europe from the beginning. I just wanted to get out of Eritrea so I went to Sudan…We decided we needed to get to Europe because friends we know living in the EU have told us that life is much better there. We didn't have a specific country in mind – just anywhere in Europe. First, we wanted to be safe and second, we wanted to build a better future for our family since we found out that we were pregnant shortly before this.

A fifth (16%) of those travelling along the Eastern Mediterranean route said that 'Europe', rather than a specific country, was their intended destination.[4] This was particularly the case for those from Eritrea and also for those with limited education, some of whom did not realise that Europe is made up of a number of different countries. For them, as for the majority of respondents, the most important priority was to reach a place in which they felt safe.

> I wanted to go to a country where we can live as human beings. I wanted to live in a country with peace and justice. I had no specific country in mind. (Afghan man aged 26)

Others, albeit a minority, told us that they wanted to go to a particular country when they left their country of origin. Those interviewed in Greece mentioned a total of 24 different countries as intended destinations, not all of which were within the EU. Germany received the highest proportion of mentions (32%), followed by Sweden (12%), the UK (6%), Switzerland (4%), Denmark and Norway (both 3%). Other intended destinations included Turkey, Greece, the Netherlands, Belgium, Finland, Austria, the United States, Italy, France, Canada, Australia, Iran, Lebanon, Russia, Saudi Arabia and Luxembourg. Our research confirms that for some people there was a perception that Germany would be the most welcoming country. This perception was particularly evident among Syrians, which accounts for the high number of mentions of Germany, but also some Afghan and Iraqi respondents.

> We want to go to Germany. Everybody is saying good things about Germany. It accepts refugees. They also told us that the asylum procedure doesn't last long there. We also heard that you get a salary and you are provided with a house if your asylum application is approved. We searched about those things on Google. (Syrian woman aged 31 travelling with her husband and three children under 3 years old)

The fact only a third of those who had a destination in mind mentioned Germany, however, suggests that other factors may be more important. Very few of our respondents mentioned the actions of Chancellor Merkel. Indeed, an analysis of 2015 arrival data shows that 'the Merkel effect', if there was one at all, can hardly be measured.[5] The number of people arriving in Greece started to increase much earlier, in spring 2015. Increased arrivals later in the year can be attributed to the deteriorating situation in Syria and neighbouring countries (discussed in Chapter Two) and the role of social networks which meant that many of those arriving were in fact travelling to join family members who had already arrived. This was reflected in the changing composition of flows seen during the fieldwork phase and is discussed further below.

Our findings for the Central Mediterranean route were very different. Here the biggest single destination choice was Libya. For example, of the 45 Gambians who participated in the research, nearly two-thirds (64%) had travelled to various countries within West Africa, starting in either Senegal or Mali, looking for work, somewhere to live and be safe. They eventually ended up in Libya because they heard along the way that it was possible to find work. A further ten respondents said that they had intended to go to Libya from the outset in order to find work. Many expected that there would be readily available employment and support from social networks of past migrants, but they also lacked an awareness of the severity of the ongoing conflict and security situation. This impression was formed through transnational networks of people who had made the journey in previous years. Smugglers would also relay information back to countries of transit and origin while offering to facilitate the journey. Of the remainder, three wanted to go to Europe (in general) because they perceived it would be safe and offer employment opportunities, three wanted to go to Italy and one wanted to go to Spain because his brother was there. A similar pattern could be seen among those from Nigeria. Of the 38 people who mentioned a destination country, more than half (58%) said that they wanted to go to Libya. The remaining respondents wanted to go to 'Europe' (7), Italy (5), 'Africa' or specific African countries (Niger, South Africa) (3) and the UK (1).

When I ran away I wanted to go to Libya, I was told there was work there in Libya...I thought there could not be worse places than Nigeria so it would be ok...I didn't know anything about the fighting. (Nigerian man aged 18 whose parents and sister were killed in Nigeria and whose brother was shot dead in Libya)

Only one-third (35%) of those who spoke about their intentions said that they had wanted to move to Europe when they set out, and even then they often had little specific knowledge about a particular

European country. Europe was, instead, imagined by many as a place of general safety and freedom, a view built up with information from people who had made the journey before as well as rumours among friends and from accessing European popular culture.

These findings challenge the idea that European asylum and migration policy is the only, or most important factor, influencing the intended destinations of refugees and migrants. There are a number of reasons why.

First, for respondents who had travelled to Greece via the Eastern Mediterranean Route the presence of family members or other social contacts (friends, acquaintances) in European countries appears to have shaped their intended destinations above all other factors. This was particularly evident among Syrian respondents, many of whom maintained almost daily contact with relatives and friends by telephone, Facebook, Whatsapp and Viber (see also Gillespie et al, 2016), but could also be seen among Afghans (travelling both directly from Afghanistan and from Iran) and Iraqis. Relationships with family and friends living in specific European countries meant that some people were sent resources for the journey and that others felt more confident about what would happen to them on arrival.

> My brother is a recognised refugee in Norway. If I succeed, I want to go there so that we can help each other. (Eritrean man aged 34 travelling alone)

It is important to note that the presence of friends or family members in particular countries was a far less significant factor shaping the intended destinations travelling through the Central Mediterranean route: very few had such close contacts informing their movements to, and within, Europe.

Second, our research, like that of Hagen-Zanker and Mallett (2016) found that refugees and migrants have limited information about specific migration policies in particular countries. Decisions about intended destinations are influenced to a far greater extent by overall perceptions about the welcome that would be given, labour market opportunities and access to education as opposed to the existence or otherwise of restrictive policies. This is reflected in the fact that many people mentioned multiple intended destinations rather than a single country, indicating that they had not yet made a decision about where they would go but were awaiting further information or advice at the point at which we interviewed them. While some respondents talked about the importance of 'allowances', housing support and access to medical treatment these factors were not as significant as the ability to secure a residence permit (often expressed as 'papers') and the right to work. Perceived opportunities for family reunification were also important. The fact that people mentioned the importance of employment opportunities does not mean that they are 'economic migrants', rather, that having lost everything, they were determined to find a place to live in which they would have the greatest opportunity to rebuild their lives. The factors mentioned as being important were related to the desire of our respondents to support themselves after arrival.

> So the last two to three months I started thinking of going to Germany. It's good there and there are jobs available. Germany has more employment opportunities than the rest of the countries in Europe. (Syrian man aged 36)

Box 4.4: Opportunities for education – and a future

Mahmod was 22 years old and living in Mosul (Iraq) where he was studying accountancy at university. In June 2014, IS took over the city. Mahmod told us that people were happy because they wanted to overthrow the government and thought that their situation would improve. Very quickly however they came to realise that IS would severely affect their quality of life and what they were, and were not, allowed to do. The university was closed down and Mahmod was no longer able to continue with his studies. He told us that he decided to leave with his younger brothers: 'My idea was to leave alone, but I took my younger brothers with me. We bought fake documents for my younger brother, which said that he was sick. So, 40 days after IS came, in August 2014, we went from Mosul to Kirkuk legally. It was easy to leave back then. Then a law which forbid leaving Mosul was implemented.

We went to a hotel in Kirkuk. We were not thinking of going to Europe yet.' Mahmod and his brothers travelled on to Baghdad where they met their father who decided to return to Mosul in order to be with their mother. Determined to continue with his studies, Mahmod submitted an application to the University of Baghdad but it was rejected. Then he went back to Kirkuk but his application to attend the university there was also rejected. After being rejected for another university course in Kurdistan, Mahmod decided to travel to Turkey and his brothers returned to Mosul to join their parents. The family tried to leave Mosul and join Mahmod in Turkey but it was too late: by that time it was nearly impossible to leave the city. Mahmod took up various jobs in Turkey but was paid very little. When his brothers joined him, it was impossible to live on a single low salary so Mahmod applied to the UN for assistance but his meetings with them were constantly postponed. He tried to find ways to travel legally to Europe in order to be able to study but it proved impossible: 'I was constantly thinking that I wanted to finish my studies. I had also applied to go to the USA, Australia or Canada through the UN. I had never thought till then to go illegally to Europe. I don't like illegal things.' After his aunt left Turkey travelling across the Aegean and through the Balkans to Austria, Mahmod decided that he and his brothers had no choice but to take the same route: 'My father sold the house that would be my present for my university graduation and he sent us the money.' They borrowed some additional money from an uncle living in Qatar and paid a smuggler to get them to Greece. From there Mahmod told us he wanted to go first to Germany and then perhaps Sweden with the aim of continuing his studies and, ultimately, securing a job to support his family.

Finally, there was significant variation in the extent to which the refugees and migrants we spoke to had information about the situation in the countries to which they were travelling. The extent to which people were able to access information about asylum and migration policies depended, in significant part, on their economic, social and cultural capital, including the ability to access online digital sources of information. In the very rapidly changing policy environment seen during 2015, it often proved difficult, even for those with smartphones, to access accurate up-to-date information. In this context decisions about intended destinations were sometimes shaped by *ad hoc* information and chance encounters from those who had already arrived in Europe or were travelling along the same route.

In the beginning, I wanted to go to Denmark, but later I changed my mind. Now I want to go to Finland...In Athens, I met a guy who lived for 10 years in Finland and he told some things about the country. That's how I changed my mind and decided to go to Finland. (Syrian man aged 25 travelling alone)

Information was also communicated to refugees and migrants by smugglers who were engaged at different stages of the journey. This is the issue to which our discussion now turns.

Notes

[1] More information at http://web.stanford.edu/group/mappingmilitants/cgi-bin/groups/view/61

[2] Iran is fighting a proxy war in Syria in support of the Assad regime and Iran's Revolutionary Guards Corp (IRGC) has recruited thousands of undocumented Afghans living there to fight in Syria since at least November 2013. See www.hrw.org/news/2016/01/29/iran-sending-thousands-afghans-fight-syria for more information.

[3] The SAWA Defence Training Center is a military camp in the Gash-Barka region of Eritrea where the Eritrean Defence Forces (EDF) recruits and national service conscripts are sent for basic military training.

[4] Not all of those who participated in the research were asked, or responded to, this question.

[5] For a detailed discussion of the 'Merkel effect', see Faigle et al (2016).

FIVE

Navigating borders and danger: the use of smugglers

Discussion of smuggling dominated the media airwaves and policy pronouncements during the 'migration crisis' of 2015. The European response emphasised the predominance of 'transnational smuggler networks' in facilitating people into Europe with proposed expanded military action to 'smash the trafficking gangs'[1] and 'disrupt' the smuggler's business model.[2] In this story, smugglers were the 'villains' who were responsible for the exploitation and the loss of life of refugees and migrants in exchange for profit. But, as this chapter will show, this perspective is an over-simplification and obscures the reasons why people engaged the services of smugglers.

Every single one of the 500 people we spoke to had utilised the 'services' of a smuggler for at least one stage of their journeys from their place of origin to the place where we interviewed them. We know that migrant and refugees' interactions with smugglers shape the routes, lengths and dangerousness of journeys (Salt and Hogarth, 2000; Van Liempt, 2007; Hernandez-Leon, 2008; Sanchez, 2015; Belloni, 2016; Tinti and Reitano, 2016). Our data presents an opportunity to elaborate on the use of smugglers across the different migration routes taken by the respondents (described in Chapter Three) to reach Greece, Italy, Malta and Turkey. Our findings also point to the need for policymakers to consider far more carefully the nuances of who smugglers are and what they do, as well as the, often intricate, relationships they develop with the people they are smuggling.

Reasons for the use of smugglers

Only a handful of respondents who crossed the Mediterranean in 2015 hired a smuggler at the point of departure to facilitate their movement *all the way* from their home country. Rather, most engaged smugglers to facilitate specific *legs* of the journey, making decisions dependent on the local context at that time. This reflects the findings of Chapters Three, Four and Six that a significant proportion of those arriving in Europe in 2015 did so after making *multiple* decisions about where, and when, to go rather than by making a singular and direct journey to Europe. The findings of our research indicate that the point at which respondents involved a smuggler to help facilitate their journeys was primarily contingent on two factors:

- whether smugglers were required to help people escape or bypass conflict, danger or persecution at home or *en route* (*Navigating danger*); and
- whether individuals could travel legally or without passing border and other controls at which travel documents and IDs were required (*Navigating border controls*).

Escaping and navigating danger

Box 5.1: Getting out: the experiences of Hayyan and his family

Hayyan was living in Daraa in Syria with his wife and two young children when they decided to escape the conflict raging around them and attempt to reach safety in Europe. Hayyan found a smuggler in Daraa, his home town, who arranged to take the family to Suwayda for US$600 per person. From there, Hayyan paid another US$1,000 in total for a different smuggler to take them through the highly dangerous city of Deir Al-Zour which was governed by IS. The family was then caught by IS. Although Hayyan's wife was wearing a niqab her hands were uncovered. Hayyan was interrogated about whether he was taking his family to Europe, a 'crime' for which Hayyan knew he and his family could be killed. Eventually the family was released and they took a bus to Aleppo. The journey, which would normally take a maximum of three days, took 13 days. From Aleppo, Hayyan and his family took a taxi to the Syrian border with Turkey. The taxi driver was the 'smuggler' and he took them to his house in a Kurdish village close to the border – Ayn al-Arab – where they stayed for one full day waiting for an opportunity to cross. The following day, the smuggler/taxi driver drove them closer to the border, where his collaborator was waiting. He asked the family for US$50 per person to help them cross into Turkey. However, after some negotiation the smuggler agreed to reduce the fee. After walking for 40 minutes, the Turkish border police caught the family but the smuggler escaped. After stealing the man's money (the equivalent of $130 in Turkish lira), the police took Hayyan and his family back across the border to Syria. Fortunately, the family were able to find another smuggler who took them successfully across the border for US$200 in total.

The *Protocol against the Smuggling of Migrants by Land, Sea and Air, Supplementing the United Nations Convention against Transnational Organized Crime* defines 'smuggling of migrants' as 'the procurement, in order to obtain, directly or indirectly, a financial or other material benefit, of the illegal entry of a person into a State Party of which the person is not a national or a permanent resident'.[3] Our findings highlight that for refugees fleeing conflict, a 'smuggler' can be substantially more than this in that smugglers also assist people to 'get out' of or 'get through' dangerous places (see also Crepeau, 2003; Gallagher and David, 2014; Düvell, forthcoming).

As we have already discussed (see Chapter Four), many of the people we interviewed were forced to leave their countries of origin and subsequently move on as a result of conflict, persecution and human rights abuse. For almost half (43%) of the people we spoke to who travelled to Europe through the Eastern Mediterranean route, smugglers enabled them to escape the conflict or persecution from state authorities in the country in which they were living. For a fee, smugglers along the Eastern Mediterranean route drove our respondents in the back of cars or old ambulances, acted as personal armed guards and guided people in the dark of night to help them escape dangerous situations.

Eritreans, Syrians, Iraqis and Afghans who had been living in Iran were the most likely to give this as a reason for engaging with smugglers. For example, Syrian interviewees who had been living in the cities of Aleppo, Daraa and Homs required the services of smugglers to escape through frontlines of fighting between Syrian government forces and rebel groups. For Iraqis and Syrians living in areas which were controlled by IS at that time (for example, Deir Al-Zor, Raqqa, Mosul), smugglers were viewed as the only safe way to escape without being detained or killed. Similarly, respondents living in IS-controlled areas of Iraq also engaged the assistance of smugglers to escape into Turkey.

Respondents who travelled along the Central Mediterranean route were less likely to pay smugglers to flee conflict or warzones. However, Eritrean respondents often engaged the services of smugglers to guide them past the attention of the Eritrean border patrols who would detain or shoot those caught trying to leave the country, or from 'bandits' in Sudan who were known for kidnapping and murder at the border (see Chapter Three).

> We chose Sudan, because it is safer for Eritreans to go there than going to Ethiopia. Crossing the borders though is very dangerous. Soldiers have been told to shoot anyone trying to cross the border. I took a cell phone to contact my friends. I didn't take any clothes except for those I was wearing, because clothes are visible and soldiers could realise that we were about to escape. I also took some food and water. (Eritrean man aged 34 travelling with his partner)

Respondents paid smugglers to help them escape from their homes, as well as at various junctures along journeys to help navigate particularly dangerous stretches. This meant that smugglers were also required to help cross physically dangerous terrain. Afghans required the help of smugglers to cross the geographically challenging and reputedly lawless

Nimroz region between Afghanistan and Iran, as well as the mountains between Iran and Turkey. In these regions people feared that they might be kidnapped or shot at by the Iranian authorities. Indeed, 17% of our respondents who travelled through Iran told us that they had seen people die there. To escape danger, smugglers divided their 'clients' into groups before starting to climb the mountains, perceiving that separating people into smaller groups would attract less attention or that if one group were caught, another would get through.

Along the Central Mediterranean route, smugglers were also vital for travelling through the Sahara Desert from Niger or Sudan into Libya. Without paying for expert knowledge and appropriate transportation, the physical expanse of the desert could simply not be traversed safely. One in five people (20%) who crossed the Sahara Desert spoke of witnessing people die there (Chapter Seven). Furthermore, without networks of contacts and resources to pay bribes, being stopped by the military or kidnapped by armed groups in the desert was a distinct risk. To avoid this, smugglers in Agadez, Niger, arranged convoys departing together to Sabha, across the border in Libya.

The journey in the Sahara was difficult and it took us 10 days. There are no roads in the desert so you need to go with a truck. (Gambian man in his 20s)

Among the most challenging terrain during the respondents' journeys was crossing the Mediterranean. By the time respondents reached the embarkation point for crossing into Europe (either Libya, Turkey or, to a lesser degree, Egypt), regardless of where they originated from or the directions their journeys had taken them, every single one of our 500 respondents sought out the services of a smuggler. In both Libya and Turkey, smugglers organised the boat, transferred individuals to the shore either by car, by van or by guided walking and otherwise managed the logistics of the departure. Respondents who had passed through Turkey referred to paying smugglers to signal the direction to navigate in, to provide a GPS system and occasionally to procure lifejackets, for which they usually paid extra. In Libya, however, the journeys of our respondents were even more difficult (see also Chapters Six and Seven). Staying in Libya was dangerous, but so was leaving due to the risk of kidnap or murder by militias, authorities, police and 'gangs'. Engaging with a smuggler to leave the country via the Mediterranean was risky, but still considered by many to be the only opportunity to leave this danger behind.

> When you enter Libya you cannot come out, they will shoot you at the border. When we passed we saw a border guard pour petrol on a black man and set fire to him. You cannot get out of Libya alive…You have to give your money to someone and hope they will take you. They tell you, you must take the boat. (Nigerian man in his 20s)

Navigating border controls

Box 5.2: Crossing the Iran–Turkey border

So, from Qom I went to Tehran by bus. The law does not allow us to move cities, but I took my risks. I spent seven hours in Tehran. The weather was rainy. The smuggler put seven people in a car. I was in the trunk. He took us to Urmia. We spent four nights there at a stable. These four nights the smugglers were going out to check whether there are a lot of Iranian soldiers at the border. A lot of people were gathered in the stable these four days. Most of them were families, all of them Afghans. They put us in small trucks and took us to a village close to the border. We spent two nights at a warehouse there. Again, we were waiting for the border to become safer. Before we started walking, other smugglers brought their own people too. Three hundred people were gathered in total. They divided us into three groups, 100 people per group. I was in the second team that started walking. The first group was arrested. Some of the people in the first group were shot. The smugglers told us so. And then we started walking. We were 15 single men, and the rest were families in my group. We were helping the families, because the route was hard. Some managed to cross the border, some others were left behind. (Afghan Hazara man aged 30 travelling with his partner and three friends)

At certain points in their journeys, people required smugglers to help them navigate border controls; to 'get in' to countries. Smugglers helped our respondents avoid police and immigration officials, either through guiding people past them, providing them with false documents or paying bribes to officials.

Paying a smuggler in order to bypass immigration controls, either in order to enter Europe, or before and even within countries, was regarded by those we spoke to as a necessity rather than a choice. One in ten of our interviewees who travelled to Europe via the Eastern Mediterranean route told us that before leaving home they had tried but failed to identify an alternative way to migrate legally through applying for a visa for a country regarded as safe (usually in Europe or North America), a UN resettlement programme or a family reunification visa. This would have allowed the respondents to travel without engaging with a smuggler. Even more – especially those originating from Syria – had *considered* applying for a visa in advance but decided that an attempt would most likely be unsuccessful, or even impossible. For Syrians and Yemenis there were, at the time that the research was conducted, no functioning embassies or consulates in their countries from which to seek a visa to travel legally to a place of safety: respondents would have had to travel to Amman or Beirut. This was largely impossible due to border closures by the Jordan and Lebanese governments (see Chapter Two). Several however expressed a wish that they could have had this option as an alternative to paying smugglers.

In other words, these people resorted to smugglers because they were unable to find ways to travel legally. A significant body of existing research describes how increased border and immigration controls together with the closure of legal migration routes fuels the need for smugglers (see, for example, Achilli and Sanchez, 2017). The United Nations Office on Crime and Drugs (UNODC) whose mandate is to tackle human trafficking refers to this as the great paradox of enhanced immigration controls (UNODC, 2011a). Indeed, the difficulty of travelling legally was clearly described by many of those we spoke to:

I didn't try to apply for visa. There are no embassies in Raqqa, and we were not allowed to go to the areas controlled by the regime. Also, women were not allowed outside their house. And I was avoiding exiting the house because I was scared. In Turkey they told me that it was hard to get a visa from the embassies there. (Syrian Kurdish man travelling with his wife, two children aged 6 and 8 and his mother)

I didn't try to apply for visa. Nobody gets a visa. I wish we could pay the embassy instead of the smuggler in order to come here. (Syrian man aged 20)

The possibility of applying for a visa in advance instead of paying a smuggler to help them travel irregularly was raised less often by those who travelled through the Central Mediterranean route. People from countries such as Eritrea, Ethiopia, Gambia, Nigeria and Ghana are routinely refused visas by European governments, meaning that this was highly unlikely to be considered an option for travel. Those who did refer to visas however talked about their high cost and/or their inability to acquire them without a lack of social connections.

We never thought about asking for a visa because it was impossible. We had to have thousands of euros deposited in a bank. They only give them to children of the rich [who are] rolling in money. Or to someone who was invited to Europe by a family member who guarantees you. If you're nobody's child you don't have a chance. Even an appointment with the agency which in turn can get you an appointment with the consulate costs more than €200, which is 400 dinars, or a good salary. (Tunisian woman aged 23)

Not all the respondents required the services of a smuggler to cross *all* national borders along their journeys. Journeys were sometimes undertaken legally, sometimes illegally, depending in part on the availability or otherwise of safe and legal routes and the documentation required to cross the borders (see Chapter Three). People told us that where borders were especially heavily guarded, there was a greater presence of smugglers offering ways to avoid controls. Conversely, some people travelled parts of their routes without the need for documents, such as when crossing borders without checkpoints on them or because they had documents which were valid for only part of their journey. For example, for those who were travelling from West Africa it was possible to relatively freely cross borders between member states of the ECOWAS (Economic Community of West African States) zone without the need to pay any smuggler until they reached Libya, Morocco or Algeria.

Smugglers were also engaged to help respondents avoid immigration officials and police *within* a country they were travelling through. This was especially the case in Iran, Turkey and Libya. In Iran, Afghan nationals engaged smugglers to escape the attention of the Iranian authorities. This was because, in addition to the discrimination, harassment and risk of forced conscription into Assad's militias in Syria (see Chapter Six), it is illegal under Iranian law for Afghans to travel from city to city within Iran, making internal travel within the country highly risky. Those who are caught risk detention or deportation back to Afghanistan even if they have lived in Iran most – or even all – of their lives (HRW, 2013).

> From Tehran we went to Urmia. We went by car. We changed five cars in order to reach Urmia [border with Turkey]. And we had to switch off our mobile phones. We had to follow these steps in order to avoid army detection. (Afghan Pashtun man travelling with his cousin)

Similarly, in Turkey, while some respondents travelled to Izmir by themselves to find a smuggler, others engaged a smuggler to take them from Istanbul to the coast. This was viewed as necessary in order to avoid the Turkish police stopping and detaining them *en route*.

The smuggler came with a coach [to Istanbul] and took us close to Izmir. And then we walked for two hours. More than 41 people in my group, three coaches in total, more than 10 hours the journey to the coast. We were hiding from the police all the time. They caught other coaches but not ours. It was like a cat and mouse game. (Syrian man travelling with wife and baby daughter)

In Libya, smugglers also organised journeys from the south of the country to the cities of the north. For many, this was similar to the desert border crossing from Agadez, crammed into the back of pickup trucks and covered with tarpaulin to avoid being identified. For others, however, the transfer from the southern cities of Al Qatrun and Sabha was often with a Libyan 'master' who took them to work in manual or domestic labour.

From Sabha, I went to Zlaten, and the journey took another two days. Another three cars with 40 people on board, closed in, under a tarp, hidden. Then they put us in a farm where we had to work. We worked for many months. We had to wash and sleep in this place that was very dirty and old. All crammed. They beat us and treated us very badly. (Malian man aged 25)

For all of those who participated in our research, smugglers were a necessity in order to either escape or to travel through dangerous situations, or to pass through border controls or otherwise heavily policed areas in order to reach a place of safety. This highlights the importance of not just looking at the motivations of smugglers, whether altruistic (Crepeau, 2003) or primarily profit-seeking (IOM, 2016d), but also understanding smuggling from the perspectives of refugees and migrants themselves.

Finding a 'good' smuggler

Box 5.3: Finding a smuggler

From Sar-e Pol we went to Mazari Sharif. We spent two days there at a park. We were waiting for two friends there but they didn't show up. Then we went to Kabul. We arrived in the morning and we left at night to Herat, close to the border with Iran. We went by bus. We stayed for a few days there. I was looking for a smuggler there. I found a smuggler and we went to stay at his place. I found him by chance when we were eating at a restaurant. We made a deal to send us to Shiraz. So from Herat we went to Nimroz. We spent three nights there at the smuggler's place. We were 60–70 people in total, all Afghans. Then we started walking. We walked for two nights and one day. (Young Afghan man travelling from Afghanistan to Greece)

Our findings also question the assumption that smugglers are always part of vast criminal networks. Instead, our research – like that of many others – has found that most of the smugglers with whom respondents came into contact were connected with local communities and accessed through friends and family social networks (also see Kyle and Koslowski, 2011). Relying on personal recommendations was the main way of finding smugglers. This was particularly the case among those interviewed in Greece. In part this was because of the illicit nature of smuggling but it was also because finding a 'good' smuggler was important to people trying to move. 'Good' is defined here as a smuggler who would be able to get people to their intended destination safely. People were putting their lives and those of their families in the hands of the smugglers. Being able to gather information on smugglers before money changed hands was therefore vital. The people we spoke to often placed high value on recommendations for smugglers from those within their social networks who had successfully (and safely) reached Europe. With limited available information, these recommendations acted as a proxy for 'trustworthiness'.

I already saved the phone numbers of three smugglers in Izmir since I was in Syria. I had found them through friends and relatives who had already done the journey earlier. It's easy to find them from mouth to mouth. (Syrian man travelling with wife and two children)

As suggested in Chapter Four, smartphones and social media apps were particularly important for those travelling along the Eastern Mediterranean route, allowing them to talk with friends and family and serving as a mode of communication to share information about smugglers. Although social media was sometimes presented as the mechanism through which smugglers were able to exploit refugees and migrants,[4] it is important to distinguish between the use of social media to find a smuggler and social media being used for the purpose of communication between friends and family about potential smugglers. Just five of the 215 people interviewed in Greece told us that they found their smuggler through an advert on a website or social media site. None of those travelling through the Central Mediterranean route had found a smuggler this way, although as with those travelling through the Eastern Mediterranean route, they did seek recommendations. In other words, social media was simply a tool through which the recommendations of friends, family members and others were communicated.

Those who were not able to find a personal recommendation for a smuggler instead had to seek them out in the various cities through which they passed. In cities with widespread smuggling activities, such as Agadez in Niger (see Chapter Three), bus stations, internet cafes, public squares, markets and 'ghettoes', 'garages' or 'foyers' were readily accessible places to locate someone who could organise the journey. For people travelling through countries such as Libya, Niger, Chad or Sudan, however, information was often scarce and rarely trustworthy. Seeking to connect with smugglers could result in being kidnapped, beaten or shot at. In many cases the urgency of leaving, particularly from the dry, barren context of Agadez or the violence and instability of Libya, led people to make their journeys with the only smugglers that they could find and were able to afford.

I paid 130,000 CFA [US$230] for the journey to Sabha and from Sabha to Tripoli was 700 dinars [US$510]…when I arrived in Agadez I met the connection man at the bus station, then stayed in the bus station…there is always a connection man in the station asking who wants to go to Libya. (Ghanaian man in his 30s)

Where possible, people asked around, usually within their own communities, for recommendations about 'good' smugglers. Because of this, they predominantly engaged with smugglers who came from the same ethnic or national backgrounds. For instance, Syrian Kurds found smugglers in Turkey from within the Syrian or Turkish Kurdish community, Afghans approached other Afghans in the Zeytinburu neighbourhood of Istanbul, and Iraqis found smugglers from among the Iraqi community in the Aksaray neighbourhood of Istanbul. Along the Central Mediterranean route, smuggling was often organised by people from a range of different countries. In Libya, the sea crossing was usually organised by Arabs but people of the same nationality as those making the journey also commonly acted as intermediaries to the smugglers. In southern Libya, for example, people from Chad, Niger, Sudan and Libya were involved in different aspects of the smuggling trade. In northern Libya, people from Ghana, Gambia, Nigeria and other countries were also mentioned. These people were able to speak the same language as the people making the journey and mediated between the respondents and the usually Arabic smugglers in Libya. We interviewed refugees and migrants who told us about the smugglers with whom they were in contact. These smugglers were often only the smuggling intermediaries (responsible for generating the 'clients') rather than individuals further up the hierarchy who might be responsible for organising smuggling networks and finance.

In Libya the pusher is a Ghanaian, he tries to push people into the sea. I stayed renting in one of his houses then he facilitates the journey. People come and take you to the waiting place. They are Libyans. (Ghanaian man aged 20)

A similar dynamic was also described in Egypt:

> We found ourselves in a closed place, 'a deposit' with about 400 people there. Each group had a supervisor for them, Syrians, Somalian, Sudanese, Egyptians, all different groups. (Syrian man aged 27)

Much attention has been devoted in recent studies (usually commissioned by European governments) to describing the nature of the 'criminal networks' of smugglers stretching out across Europe, and most often, Africa. OECD (2015) distinguishes between the various actors involved in smuggling networks according to their roles: co-ordinators, recruiter, transporters and guides and service providers and suppliers (including spotters, cashiers, chairmen). IGAD and the Sahan Foundation (2016, 18) refer to smuggling along the Central Mediterranean route as being 'controlled by sophisticated and integrated international networks that derive massive profits...formed by key individuals in communication with each other and operating mainly between Europe (notably Italy), Libya, Ethiopia, and Sudan'. Their report also refers to 'trafficking kingpins', a term popularised in the European press during 2015.

Our research found that smuggling – through intermediaries – although illicit, was often highly visible in the towns, cities and villages along the main transit routes throughout East and West Africa, as well as Afghanistan, Turkey and Greece. This highlights the ways in which local communities can end up becoming formally or informally engaged in the smuggling business, because smuggling is interconnected with a range of social and economic livelihoods and ways of living (UNODC, 2011b). For instance, during 2015 in Izmir and Van in Turkey, Agadez in Niger, or Tripoli in Libya there were local micro-economies benefiting greatly from the profit generated from the facilitation of migration. In some cases, people living in and around these cities profited from providing temporary accommodation, food and drink or useful materials such as water flasks for the desert crossing or life jackets for the sea. People who had travelled through

Istanbul and Izmir referred to the shops and offices in which they left their fees for smugglers. They typically paid US$50 commission to these small businesses and received a password, which they could give to the businesses on their arrival in Greece. This released the funds to the smuggler.

In this way, hotel, restaurant and shop owners along the migration routes all benefited from profits generated from the irregular activities associated with smuggling. In some cases, individuals in these otherwise legitimate businesses also acted more directly as intermediaries to the smugglers. Individuals living and working along the migration routes also became involved more informally. For instance, Afghan respondents who got lost in the Iranian mountains while crossing into Turkey referred to shepherds who guided them to safety for a fee. West African respondents worked on an *ad hoc* basis for truck drivers in exchange for being transported along their journeys. We even heard about a sheep farmer in Niger who guided and hosted refugees and migrants along the way in exchange for a small fee. In other cases, local police were also involved in the fringes of the smuggling business through demanding payment of bribes from smugglers (on behalf of respondents). For instance, eight of the people we interviewed in Greece referred to the Turkish police taking bribes from the drivers of the coaches which carried people from Istanbul to the coast. In Libya, this was more direct. Militia-men, as well as police and members of the Libyan army were openly involved in facilitating smuggling. Our research highlights the diversity of those whom policy makers and the media commonly refer to as 'smugglers', as well as the necessity of adjusting the assumptions underpinning policies targeted at smashing smuggling business models.

Paying for smugglers

Along the Eastern Mediterranean route, the prices paid by respondents for smugglers *before* reaching Turkey varied significantly by route and by individual case. The prices paid by Syrians to *get out of* Syria to Turkey (in some cases via Lebanon) varied significantly depending on the place of origin, whether the journey required payment of bribes to officials or non-state actors (including IS), distance and whether it involved passing through or around a conflict zone. To escape from Syria into Turkey, respondents paid between US$30 (for simply crossing the border from Syria) and US$2,600 (for a journey to Beirut and then onto Mersin by ferry with false documents). Afghan respondents paid between US$45 and US$1,300 to travel from Iran to Turkey. Respondents were often asked to pay more by smugglers on arrival than they had previously negotiated. For instance, respondents told us that smugglers in south east Turkey often charged them more on arrival if they had used donkeys on part of the journey, or if they had used a bathroom.

People often knew well in advance, however, how much they would have to pay to cross the Aegean Sea to Greece. For Syrians, Afghans and Iraqis, the prices paid to a smuggler to organise the boat trip were pretty consistent at between US$800 and US$1,400. Prices did not vary significantly if respondents travelled all the way from Istanbul with a smuggler, or directly from Izmir, although there was more variability in the group 'packages' paid for. According to the people we spoke to this was because children tended to travel for half price, or even for free if very small: this left more scope for bargaining. Group packages varied between US$2,000 for two adults and two children, US$3,500 for seven (two adults and five children), and US$6,000 for two adults and two children. Eritrean respondents paid more than other nationalities for crossing the Aegean at between US$1,000 to US$1,800. This was because Eritreans, more than any other nationality, had pre-planned and pre-booked their trips with Eritrean smugglers before leaving Eritrea or Sudan. Other nationalities were likely to find a smuggler on arrival in Izmir or at other places along the Turkish coast.

Respondents who found a smuggler in Turkey bargained with them over the size and type of the boat, how many people were on the boat and of what nationality and whether it was daytime or night-time. These factors were believed by respondents to influence their chances of arriving safely in Greece, with people paying more for larger and more stable boats, fewer people on board, and daytime departures. Unsurprisingly, people told us that they were often cheated by smugglers at this point. Those who offered to drive the boat, or who offered to find more 'clients' for the smuggler, often travelled free.

> I spent 10 days in Izmir. I was gathering information. I was sleeping in the squares. I couldn't afford a hotel room. At some point I heard that the boat driver travels for free. I knew straight away that this was my chance. I had heard that the Iraqi smugglers charge US$1,200–US$1,300 per person and that the Syrians charge US$1,000–US$1,100 per person. I met a smuggler in Basmane and told him that I know how to drive a boat and we made a deal like that free of charge. (Syrian man aged 24 travelling alone)

Respondents who arranged their journeys across the Aegean while in Turkey commonly paid the money upon their safe arrival at the intended destination. Consequently, these smugglers in Turkey arguably had a greater financial incentive to ensure that as many people as possible arrived safely in Greece.

On the Central Mediterranean route we found a wide variation in the costs of travelling and ways of paying smugglers. This reflects the broad diversity of places of origin, routes and migration dynamics that led people towards and across the Mediterranean from North Africa to Italy and Malta (see Chapter Three). Those making the crossing to Italy from Libya had three different ways of paying. First, some respondents had already organised their journey to Europe from their place of origin who paid for the journey by international transfers. Payments were often made in stages as parts of the journey were completed. This was the case for most people from Eritrea, Sudan and Ethiopia. They paid between US$1,000 and US$4,500 for the boat journey across the Mediterranean. Most commonly, the price was US$2,000.

Second, other respondents organised the sea crossing from within Libya and paid in cash prior to boarding the boat. Payments were made to 'connection men' who took them to houses by the shore to wait before departing. This was most commonly the case for people from West and Central Africa, and from Bangladesh and Pakistan. Prices varied from between 500 to 2,500 Libyan dinars (approximately US$350 to US$1,800). The most common amount was around 1,000 dinars (approximately US$700).

Third, a number of people stated that they did not pay for the journey across the Mediterranean at all. Some said that they were able to benefit from the confusion at the embarkation point to sneak into the line waiting to board the boat. It was also sometimes because 'employers' for whom the respondent had worked 'pushed' them onto the boat either as a way of paying for their labour (with the knowledge of the individual), or to avoid paying them. In Libya, the distinctions between smugglers and those who held them in forced labour conditions were not always clear to respondents.

> I sneaked onto the boat without paying – you are pushed by men with knives…I did not pay for the journey…when I took the boat there were men with guns, cutlass, pushing, there was a risk to life but I had to go, so I just went into the queue without paying and they were just counting people on. (Gambian man aged 25)

As with the Eastern Mediterranean route, prices varied according to an individual's nationality, ethnicity or language. In contrast however, prices were not set according to the type of boat which respondents set off to Italy in: respondents had no influence over this at all.

> The Gambian people arrange the people, they gather them together and bring them and put them on the boat. The Libyans arrange the boat and the motor and stand with guns to put you on the boat…I paid 600 dinars [US$440] for the boat to some Gambian people. (Gambian man in his 20s)

Box 5.4: Paying for smugglers from the Horn of Africa

Journeys in the Horn of Africa were usually organised with the support of a smuggler and the, often very high, payments were sometimes made by international transfers. Smugglers in Eritrea are expensive, and far more expensive than for other routes. Respondents travelling the Central Mediterranean route paid between US$500 and US$2,000 to travel from Khartoum, in Sudan, to Libya. Others seeking to go further paid more, such as one Eritrean man who paid US$4,000 for a journey to Italy. For those travelling the Eastern Mediterranean route, for travelling between Kassala to Khartoum (Sudan), interviewees paid between US$32 to US$4,000, with most payments made at the upper end. The border crossing between Eritrea and Sudan was the most expensive, with journeys from Kassala to Khartoum costing between US$100 and US$400. In most cases, interviewees found a separate smuggler on arrival in Kassala – usually individuals with cars – to take them to Khartoum. On arrival in Khartoum, the price of the fake documents (visa and passport) and airplane ticket to Istanbul varied between US$4,000 to US$8,000, with a mode payment of US$6,500. Another person had paid US$18,000 to reach Turkey by plane, with false documents (he was caught, however, and deported from the airport before later travelling to Europe along the Central Mediterranean route).

Despite being more expensive than the journeys made by people in West and Central Africa, these figures suggest that the land-based route through Libya was considerably cheaper for people departing from the Horn of Africa than the air-based route to Turkey and then over the Eastern Mediterranean. However, the pre-arranged costs of the journey rarely covered all the expenses. In particular, Eritreans crossing through Sudan, Chad and into Libya commonly reported being detained or kidnapped in the desert and being made to pay a ransom in order to cross the border into Libya or to continue onwards to the north of the country. This was also commonly paid by international transfers as individuals rarely took cash with them:

I crossed the border with the smugglers who wanted US$1,000, and I arrived in Khartoum. Then we slept in a house outside the city with 40 other people and we headed to Libya. I do not remember the exact place where we crossed the border. It was night, then we came directly to Tripoli...I was paying at every stop. Another US$1,000 to enter Libya and another US$500 to be freed from a police station in the south where we were arrested. We were detained for two months, until they sent me the money. (Eritrean woman aged 35 travelling with her child)

Violence at the hands of smugglers

The refugees and migrants with whom we spoke frequently referred to the violence they experienced at the hands of smugglers. This was the case on both the Central and Eastern Mediterranean routes, although for those in Libya it was not necessarily clear who was a smuggler, who belonged to a militia or who was an 'ordinary' citizen with risks perceived to come from all Libyan people. A small number of respondents took care to mention that their smugglers had been kind to them, but our respondents mostly regarded smugglers as a necessity, and often a violent and unpleasant one at that. For example, Afghans referred to the violence of smugglers who helped them cross the mountains in between Iran and Turkey. Smugglers were reported to beat those who struggled to keep up, or who made noise which threatened to bring them to the attention of Iranian solders. Afghans who crossed these mountains were terrified of both their smugglers and the Iranian soldiers while crossing the mountains.

> The smugglers didn't allow us to talk during the journey. We walked on the mountain, 31 hours in total. We spent 3 nights on the mountain. It was very dangerous there. If you slipped, you would fall down the cliff. And if the Iranian army saw, you would be shot. We were walking at nights and resting during the day. It was very cold. I didn't know that it would be that hard. My brother said that he had only walked for 5–6 hours. We arrived at a Turkish village, I don't remember its name. The smugglers beat us up there. (Young Afghan man travelling with friends)

Smugglers' actions on the beaches (in Turkey and in Libya) prior to embarkation also caused significant fear and distress among respondents.

Smugglers were most exposed to the police, coastguard or militias (in the case of Libya) while on the beaches and consequently were likely to push people onto the boats, often with guns, in order to try to speed up the process. This was the case on the Turkish beaches as much as for people leaving from Libya (see also Amnesty International, 2015). Scenes were usually extremely chaotic as people's fear came to the fore and/or they realised that they had been cheated by their smuggler.

> They put us in the boat as if we were animals. The smugglers were lifting us and throwing us in the boat. They were lifting and throwing women and children. There were five smugglers in total. Two of them were completely drunk. And they pushed our boat to leave. The smugglers were yelling at us that all of us will be arrested. (Syrian man aged 47 travelling with his wife and three children aged 12, 9 and 6)

In summary, the findings of our research challenge the story that dominated political, policy and media narratives during 2015 which suggested that the arrival of large numbers of people to Europe across the Mediterranean in 2015 was driven primarily by unscrupulous smugglers, seeking to exploit people for profit. There can be little doubt that at least some of those engaged in smuggling cared little or nothing about the lives of the people in their charge. But it is also clear that there was a much wider range of actors involved in the process than this simple narrative suggests. Smuggling activities were highly visible and often embedded within local economies along the routes to Europe. And, most importantly, in the absence of legal routes to safety and protection, people had little or no choice other than to engage these services in order to navigate themselves and their families out of danger.

Notes

[1] See, for example, BBC (2015) 'Migrant crisis: We need to 'smash' trafficking gangs – PM', www.bbc.com/news/uk-politics-34793258

[2] European Council (2015) *Council establishes EU naval operation to disrupt human smugglers in the Mediterranean*, www.consilium.europa.eu/en/press/press-releases/2015/05/18-council-establishes-naval-operations-disrupt-human-smugglers-mediterannean/

[3] Available at www.unodc.org/documents/southeastasiaandpacific/2011/04/som-indonesia/convention_smug_eng.pdf

[4] See, for example, 'For many refugees, journey to Europe begins on Facebook', *Reuters* 1 Sept 2015, www.reuters.com/article/europe-migrants-facebook-idUSL5N11735I20150901 and 'People smugglers using Facebook to lure migrants into "Italy trips"' *Guardian* 8 May 2015, www.theguardian.com/world/2015/may/08/people-smugglers-using-facebook-to-lure-migrants-into-italy-trips

SIX

Moving on

The Sudanese government was looking for illegal migrants and deporting them back to Eritrea. If we were caught and sent back to Eritrea we would get in trouble back home because we left without fulfilling our military service...If we had a real and safe possibility of staying in Khartoum, we would have done so. But there was no chance of this. (Eritrean woman aged 25 travelling with her husband)

In unpacking the journeys of refugees and migrants in Chapter Three, it was clear that many of those crossing the Mediterranean in 2015 had not travelled directly from their countries of origin but rather had left months, or even years, beforehand. Some of those who crossed the Mediterranean in 2015 had a specific destination in mind at the point of departure from their home country and had stopped for only short periods of time in order to rest, settle, work, obtain resources or connect with onward transport. Their migration to Europe can therefore be regarded as a single journey, albeit with various stops or interruptions. For many others, including Niyat, who we met earlier and who is quoted above, the situation was very different. Niyat and her husband Michael did not initially intend to travel to Europe but decided to move on from Sudan because they did not feel safe.

In this context it is important to examine the decision making of those who spent extended periods of time in a number of other countries and the reasons why they decided to continue their journeys onwards towards Europe. These reasons included a lack of protection and security, the inability to find work or access services and the need for hope – and a sense of the future – for themselves and their families.

A lack of protection and security

The findings of our research point to the importance of differentiating between the *primary drivers* of migration from countries of origin and *secondary drivers* which lead to further migration and propel people onwards from the countries to which they move. In many cases people's decision to move on was based on concerns about safety and security. For example, Syrians living in Lebanon often felt too close to the ongoing conflict at home, or feared that they might be located by Assad government officials and persecuted because of their political activities or affiliations. Political activists were the most likely to mention this. The decision to move on due to a lack of protection and security can best be illustrated through the stories of two groups of people to whom we spoke: Eritreans fleeing forced military conscription who did not feel safe in either Ethiopia or the Sudan, and people who travelled to Libya, primarily for work, but who felt that they had no choice other than to cross the Mediterranean due to the insecurity and violence that has characterised the country since 2012.

Moving on from Ethiopia and the Sudan

Almost all Eritrean refugees cross an overland border to Ethiopia or Sudan and this was also the case for our respondents. There are an estimated 100,000 Eritrean refugees living in the Sudan and a further 160,000 living in Ethiopia.[1] A growing number of Eritreans have, however, made their way to Europe and applied for international protection in 2015 (EASO, 2016b). Our research provides insights into their decisions to move on from Sudan and Ethiopia.

Some respondents expressed concerns that it was difficult to make a life in Ethiopia due to discrimination and restricted access to the labour market and therefore decided to go elsewhere on that basis. Although both Ethiopia and Sudan, working in concert with UNHCR, commonly accept arrivals as lawful or at least 'prima facie' refugees, the Ethiopian government requires nearly all refugees, including Eritreans, to live in three camps set up near their respective borders: Shimelba (established in 2004), Mai-Ayna (2005) and Adi Harush (2010). With just a few exceptions, refugees are not legally allowed to work (ODI, 2017). The difficult situation of young Eritreans living in limbo in these camps has been documented elsewhere (UNHCR, 2011). A small number of our respondents who had travelled to Ethiopia and spent time living in camps such as Adi Harush described them as 'hell', with a lack of food, no communication with family or the outside world and a lack of employment opportunities:

> I spent one year and two months in the Adi Harush refugee camp. It was organised by UNHCR, there was multiple people, many many people there…life was bad, there was a shortage of food, no communication and I had no communication with my family or the world outside. So I left the camp to go to Sudan. (Eritrean man aged 36)

Others told us that they did not feel safe in either Sudan or South Sudan. In the case of South Sudan this was due to the civil war. Although the war officially ended in August 2015, renewed fighting has since created the world's fastest growing displacement crisis with more than 1.6 million people being forced to leave their homes (UNHCR 2017).

> I went to Sudan and worked. I was doing pretty well. Five months ago, I had to leave because of the civil war and went to find my way to Europe. (Eritrean man aged 44 travelling alone)

For those respondents who travelled to Sudan, however, their primary concern was that they could be arrested and deported back to Eritrea to face indefinite military conscription:

> I needed to leave Eritrea, but Sudan is not a safe place either. There is contact between the Eritrean and the Sudanese government and there was a huge risk that we were deported to Eritrea. (Eritrean man aged 34)

These concerns are well-founded. There are reports that the Sudanese government itself, sometimes through its notorious Janjaweed militias, has been arresting Eritrean refugees and deporting them back to Eritrea, where a dire fate awaits them (HRW, 2017).

Other Eritrean respondents similarly described how they had tried to make a life in other countries – including Uganda, Kenya, Chad, Egypt and Tunisia – before deciding to cross the Mediterranean to Europe. In almost all these cases we heard vivid descriptions of the challenges of living in countries in which there is both conflict and insecurity and few, if any, rights for non-citizens.

Life in Libya and drivers of onward movement

In Chapter Two we described the deteriorating situation in Libya and how this contributed to the increased arrival of refugees and migrants, particularly since 2011 (see also Box 2.1). Libya occupies a hugely important position in migration patterns towards Europe. The vast majority of those we interviewed in Italy and Malta had departed on boats from Libya and the country has been located on international migration routes as a country of destination as well as of transit for people heading to Europe for many years. The country has also become a central part of efforts to establish a new governance of migration in the region, with increasing collaboration between European and Libyan partners (see Chapter Eight). This makes understanding the complex dynamics at play in Libya particularly pressing.

The people we spoke to described life in Libya as violent, chaotic and unpredictable. In Chapter Four we also saw how many of those who had been living in Libya before crossing the Mediterranean had originally moved there in order to work. In this they were following a well-trodden path for those from both West as well as East Africa who lacked employment opportunities at home. It was only once people arrived in the country that they became fully aware of the extent to which the situation had deteriorated there and the consequent risks that they faced to their lives. Understanding the experiences of refugees and migrants travelling through the Central Mediterranean route therefore requires an analysis not only of the situation in the countries from which they originate but also of their experiences in Libya. These experiences mean that even though the initial decision to migrate may have been motivated primarily by economic factors, many of those arriving in Italy and Malta decided to leave Libya due to factors that are more typically associated with forced migration.

One of the strongest themes to emerge from the stories of those who lived in Libya was the extent of kidnapping, either in order to secure a ransom from friends and family for a person's release or as a mechanism for enforced labour (slavery). The smuggling trade into and through Libya has been increasingly interlinked with the ongoing power struggles among regional and tribal factions. Kidnappings for ransom, selling migrants for forced labour and organising people smuggling have provided major sources of funds for armed groups which compete for control over Libyan territory (Micallef, 2017). As a result, it is often difficult to distinguish between militias, smugglers, security forces or policemen and at times they all seem to play a role in carrying out kidnappings, putting people into forced labour and facilitating onward journeys.

Of those respondents who travelled via the Central Mediterranean route, 20% referred to either experiences of being kidnapped or knowing others who had been kidnapped during their journey to Europe. Among Gambians and Eritreans this figure rose to more than 30%. There were numerous reports of successful and attempted kidnappings, often at gunpoint. Often respondents would be beaten or tortured during the telephone call made to demand ransom to increase the possibility that the end of the line would agree to pay (see also HRW, 2014).

> Nobody could pay for me so I was put in prison. I was there for six months. Then they released me...when you go through the Sahara you are put in prison until you pay, they beat you until you pay...they call you family and your family hears you shouting in pain in the telephone. (Eritrean man aged 36)

Our research also supports emerging evidence that a market for what is sometimes referred to as 'slave labour' has emerged in Libya (Micallef, 2017), with refugees and migrants being treated as a commodity to be exploited:

> There were 50 of us in a jeep who crossed the desert and we got to Sabha. Then they arrested us and took us to a prison where we spent two weeks. We were sold as slaves to a Libyan man who brought us to work in a marble quarry. I drove a forklift to move the stones. They did not pay us. I worked there two months. We revolted and were beaten. (Malian man aged 21)

Violence was not limited to kidnapping and forced labour: it was a feature of everyday life. For most of those who travelled through Libya, gunfire could be heard daily and armed street gangs were said to pose a frequent threat.

> This year some people came when I was at work, six people, and they said 'money, money!' I had nothing and tried to run, and they stabbed me in the chest. I could not go to hospital because in hospital they kill you in Libya. (Ghanaian man aged 25)

Box 6.1: Between the devil and the deep blue sea: the decision to leave Libya

Lamin was a nurse in the Gambia. He had to leave his home when a political faction with which he was affiliated was outlawed. He lost his job and feared for his life. Lamin travelled initially to Senegal but felt unsafe and after nine months moved on to Bamako in Mali. Realising that there were no job opportunities in Bamako and that few people spoke English, Lamin decided to move to Libya where he lived for almost two years. Lamin found it difficult to recall his time in Libya. First he lived in a small village near Sabha and things were okay but 'at some point everything changed. The Arab people would take you to work but sometimes don't pay'. Fighting spread to towns and villages, no longer only between rival militia. It became dangerous to go out in the evening. Then Lamin was offered work elsewhere: 'One day a man said there's a big project, big work, so I put my things in the car and he drove me off and put me in prison. It was a kidnapping', he explained. Lamin spent nine months in prison. '[In the prison] you work for them, when somebody dies you have to move the body for them, they take you and tell you to throw the body in the ditch. It is inhuman.' Eventually Lamin was able to escape and travelled to Tripoli. He worked for a while and was able to get enough money to eat but it was a hand-to-mouth existence. He heard of an Arab man in Zuwara who organised boat crossings. He recounted the encounter in detail: 'It was a one-hour drive to Zuwara. The Arab man was a family man, a big man, he had organised trips for a long time. In the place where we were all gathered to wait for work the Arab came with some food and water. He came in a car. His son, a small boy, signalled to come over.' Lamin recalled a crowd quickly forming around the man and became anxious that he might once again be kidnapped but he felt that he had no choice other than to risk the dangerous journey across the Mediterranean: 'Some people wanted to go but others were afraid of the risk. But even just sitting there is a risk, sometimes they shoot for no reason. He [the smuggler] told us, Libya is not safe for you people, if you stay here you will all die.' And so Lamin decided to leave.

For the refugees and migrants with whom we spoke, the decision to cross the sea needs to be interpreted in the context of these experiences. Many of those we spoke to had already witnessed the death of fellow travellers prior to reaching the sea. In our interviews, 72% of the experiences in which people had directly witnessed or heard of deaths since leaving their places of origin occurred not at sea, but on land. Over a quarter (27%) of people saw or heard about someone dying while they were in Libya. For many the risks posed by moving onwards towards Europe were overshadowed by those that they would face if they were to go back the way they had come or, particularly in the case of Libya, if they were to stay where they were.

> I didn't want to be in Libya anymore, it was dangerous to me…I spoke to a friend, a man from Mali…He told me that it was better to die at sea, free, than with a bullet in my head here in Libya. (Gambian man aged 20)

The inability to work or access services

It is also clear from our research that many of those who left situations of conflict often found themselves in very difficult economic circumstances in Jordan, Lebanon, Turkey, Iran and elsewhere as a result of limited rights, exploitation by employers and discrimination in the labour market (and beyond). A third (34%) of respondents interviewed in Greece, for example, moved on for what might typically be understood as economic reasons: they were running out of money, found it impossible to secure employment or were working long hours for very little pay. Many had been living in camps or urban settings in Lebanon and Jordan (Box 6.2). Others had been trying to make a living in Turkey. Some had travelled initially to Israel in order to work but had subsequently been 'voluntarily returned' to Rwanda from where they had travelled onwards to Uganda, Turkey and, ultimately, Greece where we met them.

Box 6.2: Life in Badawi camp, Lebanon[2]

I was living in Damascus, in Yarmouk Camp. Fifty years ago it was a camp and later became a proper neighbourhood. We had to leave because they started bombing houses and we have wives and children. We were scared. I was working till my last day there, but we couldn't stay because of my wife and children. So I took my family and went legally to Lebanon, Trablous. We stayed at Badawi refugee camp in Trablous. In the beginning there was help there, we didn't have to spend a lot there, the cost of living was not high. We had to find a house. We found one for US$200 rent. The initial price was US$300, but they made us a better offer because of my kids. I was working as a builder there but I started running low on money. They were paying me less than they agreed. I worked for two-and-a-half years like that. I wasn't satisfied with my life and salary there. Everybody is exploiting you there when they realise that you are Syrian. Two-and-a-half years later I decided to leave the country but didn't know where to go. The borders were closed. I stayed for one more year there jobless. There was an organisation there, UNRWA, which has been helping Palestinians for 50 years. We were receiving assistance from them. I was receiving US$200 per month from this organisation as an assistance. But things started deteriorating in Lebanon, and the organisation which was helping us stopped providing us assistance. This is why we decided to do this journey now. (Syrian Palestinian family with three children aged 10, 8 and 7 years old)

Key drivers of onward migration from Turkey

In 2015, when the research for this book was undertaken, Turkey was already host to more than two million Syrian refugees who had arrived in the country in growing numbers since the beginning of the conflict March 2011. As of April 2017, Turkey was host to just under three million Syrian refugees, as well as others from Iraq, Afghanistan, Eritrea and other countries, making it the country hosting the largest number of refugees for the second consecutive year.[3] The unregistered refugee population may mean that the true figure is even larger. Turkish reception policies at the outset were predicated on the assumption that the conflict would come to a swift conclusion, allowing the displaced Syrians to return home, but as conditions continued to deteriorate in Syria and hundreds of thousands of people started to cross the Aegean to Greece it became increasingly clear that a shift in policy was needed to encompass longer-term solutions (İçduygu, 2015).

One of the main difficulties facing Syrian, and other, refugees living in Turkey has been that the country maintains a geographical reservation on the Refugee Convention. This means that those from outside Europe are excluded from full refugee status (2013 Law on Foreigners and International Protection (LFIP), art. 61). Syrians are excluded from asylum procedures (DGMM, 2016b) and instead dealt with under provisions for temporary protection (LFIP, art. 91). A lack of clarity around the definition of 'temporary' makes this a precarious status. All others are dealt with under provisions for asylum seekers and, if approved, granted a conditional refugee status (LFIP, art. 62). People in this group are expected to be resettled or to receive subsidiary protection (LFIP, art. 63). However, the waiting time for the first interview was seven years in 2015 and had increased to eight years by 2016. This left people in periods of prolonged limbo. The demand for resettlement vastly outstripped the supply of places. Legal provisions as well as social services for unaccompanied children minors were insufficient. There were also concerns about refoulement which undermines the safety of refugees in Turkey (COE, 2016).

As a consequence, a large proportion of Syrians, Iraqis, Afghans and other refugees living in Turkey suffer from a precarious immigration status, severe poverty and a lack of prospects for improvements in their living conditions. These conditions continue to represent pressures for onward migration. Syrians and some Iraqis can be accommodated in camps but there are only around 247,000 places, which represents just 8.2% of the total (DGMM, 2016a). All others have to identify and pay for their own accommodation which is usually sub-standard and over-crowded in basements, sheds or derelict houses. Until January 2016, all asylum seekers were excluded from the labour market and the new 'Regulation on Work Permit of Refugees Under Temporary Protection' did not yet substantially change this.[4] Therefore, Syrians and other refugees, if they can find employment, normally work in low paid sub-standard jobs. Many report severe exploitation and unpaid wages. Child labour is widespread (COE, 2016). By law Syrians have access to some key social provisions including healthcare and education. However, often this cannot be realised due to lack of resources, staff or interpreters. For instance, 42% of Syrian children do not attend school (UNICEF, 2017). And until autumn 2016, almost no benefits were paid. A significant number of CSOs, however, provide services and fill some gaps. The evidence in relation to equality and discrimination is mixed: some Kurds chose to live in Kurdish neighbourhoods and enjoy community support, others refer to discrimination of Kurds in Turkey and do feel not safe.

In the concluding chapter of this book we reflect on some of the policy developments that have taken place since 2015 in an effort to address the situation in Turkey, including the agreement that was signed between the EU and Turkey to stop flows across the Aegean. It is questionable whether these policy developments have significantly improved the lives of Syrian refugees living in Turkey. What is clear however is that the inability to find reasonably paid work and to access services such as education and healthcare is central to understanding the dynamics of migration across the Aegean. With the passage of time, and in the absence of a resolution to the conflicts in their home countries, respondents told us that they had grown increasingly concerned about the impacts on their families, and especially their children, many of whom had been out of school for many years or had health issues. The arrival of significant numbers of people in Greece in 2015 therefore raises important questions about the long-term situation for refugees and migrants living in countries such as Jordan, Lebanon and Turkey, some of whom decided to cross the Mediterranean in 2015.

> Back then I just wanted to leave Syria. I wasn't thinking of going to Europe. I had an acquaintance there. In two or three days I found a job as a waiter in a restaurant in Istanbul. I worked there for two months but I didn't get paid. I left that job for another one. I was working from seven in the morning until midnight for 1,000 liras [US$275], and I was sleeping in the restaurant too... My wife joined me in Istanbul. We rented a house. At some point, our daughter got ill and we couldn't take her to the hospital because we were illegal. This is when we decided to leave Turkey. (Syrian man aged 29 whose pregnant wife and 1-year-old child were living in Sweden)

The need for hope – and a future

This chapter has addressed the reasons why people decided to move on and suggests that these decisions were associated with a lack of security or the inability to make a living and build a new life. Running through the accounts we heard were feelings of hopelessness and a sense that some of the things that were lacking in their lives – such as access to employment, affordable healthcare or education for children – could be secured elsewhere. This is perhaps best illustrated by the situation of Afghans living in Iran.

Afghans in Iran: 'They treat us like dogs'

> I could have been naturalised in Iran in the past, but I was expecting that the situation in Afghanistan will get better, so I decided not to. In Iran I was afraid to go out. They are treating Afghans as if they are dogs. (Afghan man aged 32 travelling with his sister and her husband)

The year 2015 saw a significant increase in applications for international protection from those with Afghan nationality, with the number of asylum applications more than quadrupling to 178,200,[5] making Afghans the second largest group seeking protection in Europe (EASO, 2016b). During the same year the Afghan refugee population worldwide was estimated to be around 2.7 million, constituting the second-largest refugee population in the world, having lost the dubious title of top refugee-producing country to the Syrians the previous year (UNHCR, 2016).

The main reasons for the increase in asylum applications to Europe are two-fold. First, although it has been beset by conflict for nearly 40 years, the on-going exodus (not only) to Europe reflects an unchanged – and partially even worsening – general security situation in the country (Ruttig, 2017). This includes growing involvement of IS, alongside the Taliban, resulting in higher casualties among Afghan forces and groups such as the ethnic minority, Hazara, who have been specifically targeted because they are mainly Shia.[6] At no time since the start of the 2001 US invasion of Afghanistan have the Taliban controlled more territory in the country.[7]

Understanding the movement of Afghans to Europe, however, also requires us to look at the limited opportunities for meaningful, long-term protection in the region. Nearly half (43%) of our Afghan respondents left Afghanistan more than five years prior to their interview with us and of these a significant proportion (39% of the total) had been living outside Afghanistan, mainly in Iran, for more than ten years. Seven respondents had not been to Afghanistan for more than 20 years, and some for as long as 35 years. Nearly a quarter (23%) had never been to Afghanistan at all, having been born in either Iran or Pakistan. This means that two-thirds (66%) of those we spoke to had either never been to Afghanistan or had not lived there for a considerable period of time.

In 2015 Iran was the fourth largest refugee-hosting country in the world with nearly one million registered Afghan refugees and an estimated two million more who are undocumented (UNHCR, 2015). Many arrived following the US-led invasion of 2001 but there is a long history of migration to the country (PRIO, 2004). Although Iran has been praised by UNHCR for hosting more than 1.5 million Afghan refugees with no assistance from the international community,[8] there are an estimated 1.4 to 2 million undocumented Afghans living in the county with extremely limited rights. There is evidence of severe maltreatment of Afghans, including summary deportations, physical abuse at the hands of security forces, limited job opportunities outside menial labour, and restricted access to education (HRW, 2013). Newly arrived Afghans cannot regularise their status. The majority of documented Afghans are those who had been registered as refugees in Iran between 1979 and 1992, and were then able to re-register under the new system that was established. At the same time undocumented Afghan refugees living in Iran are increasingly being forced to return to Afghanistan even though, in some cases, they have never lived there.

For many Afghans living in Iran, particularly those from the ethnic Hazara minority, experiences of severe discrimination, the absence of citizenship rights and a lack of education for children combined with anxieties about what would happen to them if they were to return to Afghanistan and information from others that they might be able to secure protection in Europe, influenced the decision to move on.

I was forced to work since I was very young because my father passed away. I was not happy with my life in Iran. I was tired of my life. There was no justice for me because I was Afghan. When I was in school, a teacher of mine told me that I am not entitled to speak because I am a guest in the country. Afghans do not have a future in Iran. (Afghan woman aged 21 travelling with her husband, son aged two-and-a-half years, brother and cousin)

Meanwhile the ongoing conflict in Syria has had ripple effects across the region. According to HRW (2016b), since at least November 2013, Iran's Revolutionary Guards Corps (IRGC) has recruited thousands of undocumented Afghans living there to fight in Syria, some of whom have reported coercion. This was the experience of some of the young Afghan men to whom we spoke.

They sent me to Syria, together with many other young people. They told that [we] will fight there just for three months and then we will return to Iran and get a permanent residence permit. But when I returned they fooled me and they just gave a one-month residence permit. They told me that I have to go back to Syria, and fight for three more months there. Long story short, I went two more times in Syria. Yet, they never gave me a permanent residence permit. When they told me to go for a fourth time, I accepted their offer, but I decided to flee. So I fled as fast as I could and I took my mother with me. (Hazara Afghan man aged 20 travelling with his fiancé, father, mother, two brothers and two nephews)

It is clear that rather than leaving their homes and 'heading to Europe', many refugees and migrants in fact spent months or even years living in neighbouring or other countries within which they lived before they decided to make the journey to Europe. The vast majority of people remain there. But for some, the situation of insecurity, inability to make a living and secure access to rights and the economic and social opportunities with which they are associated, as well as an overwhelming sense of hopelessness and a concern about what the future held, led them to risk everything and attempt to cross the Mediterranean. Our discussion now turns to people's experiences on the journey and what happen to them when they arrived on the shores of Europe – and subsequently.

Notes

[1] See www.unhcr.org/protection/operations/524d87ac9/sudan-fact-sheet. html and http://et.one.un.org/content/dam/unct/ethiopia/img/Document%20 cover%20pages/UNHCR_Fact_Sheet_June2016.png

[2] Badawi camp in the north of Lebanon is not much different from any other Palestinian refugee camp in the country in that it lacks any effective infrastructure or services, the crowded streets are narrow and filthy with tiny shops crammed along both sides. The population of the camp fluctuates depending on the security situation in the region with many of those living in the camp having been displaced on multiple occasions. More at www. washingtonreport.me/2007-september-october/displaced-palestinians-at-lebanons-badawi-camp-dream-of-refugee-camp-home%C2%9D.html

[3] Figures correct as of 27 April 2017, http://data.unhcr.org/syrianrefugees/ country.php?id=224

[4] See Anadolu Agency (2017) 'Turkey issues work permits to over 73,500 foreigners' 18 Jan 2017, http://aa.com.tr/en/economy/turkey-issues-work-permits-to-over-73-500-foreigners/729836

[5] http://ec.europa.eu/eurostat/documents/2995521/7203832/3-04032016-AP-EN.pdf/

[6] See, for example, www.theguardian.com/world/2016/jul/23/hazara-minority-targeted-by-suicide-bombs-at-kabul-protest and www.hrw.org/ news/2016/10/13/afghanistans-shia-hazara-suffer-latest-atrocity

[7] www.nytimes.com/2016/10/06/world/asia/afghanistan-eu-refugees-migrants.html?_r=0

[8] 'UN hails Iran for keeping doors open to refugees', 16 March 2017, www. presstv.ir/Detail/2017/03/16/514536/UNHCR-Iran-Afghan-Refugee-Migrant

SEVEN

Across the sea... and beyond

In 2015 the political, policy and media focus was very much on the dangerous and difficult journey across the sea. Even today this largely remains the case. In this chapter we explore our respondents' experiences of the sea crossing and also what happened when they arrived on the shores of Europe. Just as the sea crossing was not the beginning of the story, neither was it the end. Although the focus shifted towards the end of 2015 onto the movement of people up through the Balkans to the countries of Northern Europe, there were also other movements taking place which are rarely acknowledged or spoken about in policy debates. These included the movement of refugees and migrants from Greece to countries other than those in Northern Europe, including Italy and Malta, typically seen as arrival rather than destination countries. In addition, European countries also created their own movement, largely through enforced returns under the Dublin Regulation which continued despite media stories to the contrary.[1]

Crossing the Mediterranean

It is too risky to go back across the desert. It is better to cross and risk your life in the sea than go back. (Nigerian man aged 26)

The decision that refugees and migrants took to risk their lives and, in many cases those of their children, by boarding a boat to cross the Mediterranean becomes easier to understand in the context of knowing what happened to them before they reached the sea. As is clear from preceding chapters, journeys over land were dangerous, with danger coming from a variety of different sources: from smugglers, from state officials, from challenging terrain and from 'bandits'.

More than three-quarters (76%) of those interviewed in Italy and Malta said that they had been on the receiving end of physical violence from someone during their journeys before reaching the Mediterranean. Almost a third (29%) had witnessed the death of a fellow traveller, sometimes a family member, along the way. People from West African countries (Gambia, Nigeria, Senegal, Ghana and Côte d'Ivoire) experienced the highest levels of violence *en route*, perhaps reflecting the greater length of their journeys and greater number of border crossings. Along the Central Mediterranean route, most reports of violence occurred in Algeria, Niger, Chad, crossing from Eritrea into Sudan and, overwhelmingly, Libya.

A smaller proportion, around 40%, of those travelling via the Eastern Mediterranean route had experienced physical violence during their journeys: 8% had witnessed the death of a fellow traveller. As with those who were interviewed in Italy and Malta, some routes and locations were perceived by interviewees as being more dangerous than others. Afghans were the most likely to experience dangerous and frightening journeys. Around half (51%) of Afghans travelling through Iran experienced violence, most notably at the hands of state agents (police, border guards and the military).

Nonetheless, and regardless of what had happened on the journey across land, the journey over the sea was almost always frightening and difficult, particularly for those who had never previously seen the sea, or travelled on water. Those who had money and were travelling along the Eastern Mediterranean route negotiated with smugglers (sometimes successfully, sometimes not) to avoid travelling at night, to travel with fewer passengers in each boat and in more secure, seaworthy boats in order to mitigate the risks (see Chapter Five). Those travelling along

the Central Mediterranean route had substantially less opp
to negotiate with smugglers. Everyone was acutely conscious ᴏₗ .
risks they faced, with many expressing a belief that their chances of
successfully reaching Europe would, ultimately, 'be in God's hands'.
People's faith (predominantly Islam or Christianity), played an
important role in helping them to deal with fear, anxiety and trauma.

> I really wanted to die [before they rescued us]. Gradually we all
> wanted to die. God is our only rescue. It was God who saved
> us. He rescued us and tied the rope [of the rescue ship] to the
> boat. (Nigerian man in his 20s)

Smugglers were also aware of the risks and that successful crossings
often depended upon the search and rescue (SAR) activities of
the Greek and Italian coastguards, as well as those of CSOs and of
coordinated efforts by fellow travellers on social media.

> I had found a Facebook group, where you can post your
> whereabouts in the sea in case you are lost, or in case you have
> a problem with your boat. It's called Iraqi Help Group. You can
> post your location on the group, and they call the coastguard in
> order to rescue you if anything goes wrong. Our journey lasted
> two and a half hours. For two and a half hours I was updating
> our location on that Facebook group. And the group called the
> Red Cross in order to help us. (Iraqi man aged 28 travelling
> with his 4-year-old son)

While this was the case for both routes, it was particularly evident in
relation to the crossing from Libya to Italy. Just over one in ten of those
interviewed in Greece were rescued by the coastguard or by CSOs in
the Aegean Sea. In contrast, all those who crossed the Mediterranean
from Libya were rescued at sea and taken to ports in southern Italy
or Malta (see Chapter Two). Rescues were mounted by the Italian
coastguard, by commercial ships, and by CSOs such as MSF, MOAS
and others. The boats working in Central Mediterranean waters carried

doctors and paramedics which were essential due to the, sometimes desperate, condition of those rescued.

> At a moment where we have more than 400 people on board for like 48 hours, we need people to take care of them both from a medical point of view because many of them may have scabies or having suffered beatings, [there may be] pregnant women, you can have everything. (Respondent working on a CSO rescue boat)

Box 7.1: Rescued at sea: the story of Joseph

Joseph, originally from Ghana, travelled on a boat which got lost in the Mediterranean. The passengers on the boat called the rescue telephone number which they had been given by the smugglers but there was no answer and the battery was getting weaker so they turned the phone off for a while to try and conserve power. From 6am to 3pm that day they sat on the boat with no water or food: 'Even the young guys had no strength and could not pull themselves off the floor.' Some of the men on the boat demanded that the captain take them to dry land anywhere, even Tunisia, but Joseph argued with them saying that if the captain was lost it would be impossible for him to get to Tunisia and even if they did then they would be killed. By this stage a level of despair had started to affect many of those on the boat: 'We were all praying and weeping, asking God to push us to Italy.' He told us that while Gambians 'live in water' very few Ghanaians have seen boats bigger than canoes. For Joseph, seeing only the sea and no land was a new and terrifying experience. The sea was also very rough at times. When they switched the phone back on at the end of the day they found a signal which Joseph attributed to God's intervention, and they managed to speak to the man who had organised the journey. He gave them an alternative number to call for the rescue, which they did. Joseph described his relief at being rescued: 'My happiest day in my life was not when my mother gave birth to me but when I saw a helicopter and we knew we had a 50 per cent chance to live.' Forty-five minutes later a ship with a Swiss flag appeared to rescue them and take them to Italy.

While sea crossings were much shorter between Turkey and Greece, the people we spoke to were no less traumatised by their experiences at sea. Sometimes this was because of unseaworthy inflatable dinghies which took on water, capsizing with all those on board having to swim for land. Other times, the fear arose from the actions of police, coast guards and others including vigilante groups, who tried to stop their crossings, often violently. As was noted in Chapter Five, smugglers' actions on the beaches also caused a significant amount of fear and distress.

Deaths at sea

Box 7.2: David and Loli: detention, despair and death

David was just 16 years old when he left his home in the Gambia in April 2014 with his younger sister Loli. David and Loli went first to Senegal 'because it was the closest' and stayed there for three weeks in a house with other Gambians. David decided to move on when he could not find work, travelling through Mali to Burkina Faso and subsequently Niger. David and Loli stayed in Niger for around two weeks before taking a pickup truck with around 30 other Africans. The journey across the Sahara took four days. When David arrived in Libya he realised that it was very dangerous. He worked in construction before moving to Tripoli, but he and Loli were arrested and put in prison:

> The conditions were terrible in the prison and my sister was very upset. They released us after two days but they told us that we needed to get out of their country, and that if we tried to stay they would kill us. They brought us down to the boats and I thought better that I die on the boat with my freedom than be captured again by the Libyans. They pushed me onto the boat but tried to keep my sister with them as they said she was too young to travel and that she may not survive the journey. This was very upsetting for both of us. I told them I'd rather die than leave her here and that there was no way we would be separated. My sister was crying as well saying the same thing. Eventually they let her on and they pushed our boat out to sea.

David told us that the boat was driven by another passenger who didn't know the way: 'We spent eight days on the water with no food or water. We began to drink the sea water. This made us very ill. Our heads started to get dizzy...' Loli died on the journey but David was rescued and taken to Malta, which is where we met him. When we asked him if he intended to travel to Europe when he and Loli left Gambia or if he knew about the rescue boats, David told us:

I never intended to come to Europe, I just wanted to leave my life in Gambia, went to Senegal, and the situation wasn't good, same in all African countries. I had no idea about Europe...We weren't told about the rescue boats, we were just sent to the sea. We all feared that we would end up in Libya again, we would all be killed.

David spent four days in hospital when he arrived in Malta before being sent to Safi detention centre for three months. He was subsequently granted refugee status.

From 2014 to the end of 2016 over 500,000 people travelled to Europe via the Central Mediterranean route from North Africa towards Europe, arriving predominantly in Italy. More than one million people made the Eastern Mediterranean crossing from Turkey to Greece. Over the same period of time, the deaths of 11,910 people trying to make the journey have been recorded.[2] The actual figure is probably much higher. The deaths of those crossing the Mediterranean causes deep distress for their families, who often do not know the fate of their loved ones and are unable to see their bodies.[3] It has also led to repeated calls for urgent action from politicians, policymakers and CSOs across Europe (see, for example, Amnesty International, 2015; 2015; MSF, 2016; 2017). In April 2015 the deaths of up to 1,200 people at sea when the two boats carrying them sank 60 miles off the coast of Libya was followed by a series of high-level summits among EU leaders to address the 'crisis'. Later in the year, media coverage of the 'crisis' would be dominated by pictures of the body of the small boy Aylan Kurdi, washed up on a Turkish beach after the boat in which his family was trying to reach Greece sank. His mother and brother also drowned. Reducing deaths at sea has since repeatedly been employed as a justification for stopping people from moving altogether, whether in the form of the EU–Turkey agreement in the Eastern Mediterranean, training the Libyan coastguard to intercept boats in the Central Mediterranean or criminalising privately-owned and run SAR operations (see Chapter Eight).

The general data on deaths in the Mediterranean masks a range of important variations, however, which in turn point towards significant differences in migration dynamics on the two routes. Although the majority of the arrivals to Europe by sea during 2015 were through the Eastern Mediterranean route, by far the greatest number of deaths was recorded in the Central Mediterranean. From 2014 to 2016, 1,299 deaths were recorded on the Eastern crossing. On the Central crossing 10,611 deaths were recorded over the same period. During 2016 the proportion of people drowning compared with those who successfully reached Greece, Italy or Malta (the 'death rate') rose on both routes. On the Eastern Mediterranean, the likelihood of dying more than doubled. Whereas during the peak of arrivals of people on the Greece islands in 2015 one death was recorded for every 1,098 people who arrived across the Eastern Mediterranean route, in 2016, this increased to one death for every 420 people who successfully made it to Greece. On the Central Mediterranean route, there was one death for every 55 arrivals in 2015.[4] In 2016, this rose to one person for every 40 reaching Italy.

The higher death toll on the Central Mediterranean route can be attributed to various factors. One reason is that the journey is much longer than the relatively short crossing between Turkey and Greece. Whereas Turkish smugglers used inflatable dinghies which could be rapidly inflated and prepared on beaches to transport just tens of people at a time, smugglers in Libya and Egypt used mainly old wooden fishing boats with the potential to carry hundreds of people at once. These larger boats carry greater potential for higher death tolls in case of sinking and pose the risk of asphyxiation from engine fumes for those loaded into the hold below deck.

The danger associated with the journey across the Mediterranean therefore reflects a complex relationship between migration dynamics, border control policies and smuggler strategies. The impact of policies and smuggler strategies on the riskiness of journeys can be seen in both routes. On the Central Mediterranean route some smugglers chose to put less fuel in a boat in order to reach military and humanitarian missions in international waters instead of crossing all the way to Italy. On the Eastern Mediterranean route, many of the CSOs we spoke to expressed concern that increased efforts to reduce the number of boat crossings to Greece were leading smugglers to send boats at more dangerous times, for example at night or in poor weather conditions, when rescue attempts were less likely to be successful. More recent evidence suggests that a similar strategy to avoid detection by increased security patrols at sea is being employed by Libyan smugglers, who during 2016 and 2017 have increasingly used dinghies and sent multiple boats at the same time.[5] The implications are discussed in Chapter Eight.

Arriving on the shores of Europe

Although the sea crossing was only a small part of the journey to Europe, it clearly took its toll. Refugee and migrants arrived in Europe exhausted but also relieved to have reached a place of safety and somewhere they would find protection and support for themselves and their families (see Chapter Four). Tears of joy could often be seen alongside distressed and traumatised faces on Greek beaches and Italian quaysides.

> When we arrived I just said 'Thank God!' I just thanked God. Many people lose their life, I could lose my life but God saved me. (Gambian man aged 31)

In Chapter Two we outlined the divergent policy response to the arrival of refugees and migrants in Europe, highlighting a more 'managed system' in Italy and a more chaotic reception context in Greece. Some of the arrival procedures in Italy were rapid and people were transferred from boats to reception centres around the country quickly and efficiently. In these cases, the experience for most of those we spoke to was an orderly, if confusing, process through which they were shuffled in an exhausted state.

> They give us slippers, and then we sit, and then they give us a red card, and then we sit, and then they give us water and we sleep. (Gambian man aged 19)

People interviewed in Italy tended to remember few details of disembarkation itself. However, many respondents did speak of procedural inconsistencies on quaysides and in the moving of people to reception facilities. They spoke of an array of organisations waiting for them and of receiving differential levels and types of information about their rights and the requirements of the reception system. Some people described speaking to people with 'blue vests'. Blue vests are worn by representatives from UNHCR and were seen as an opportunity to claim asylum. But they are also worn by Frontex representatives, who often sought to distinguish 'economic migrants' from 'refugees' on the basis of nationality and were eager to collect information about the smugglers who had organised the journey. Those arriving after the sea journey were generally unaware of the role of Frontex. This confusion between officers responsible for protection and policing had significant implications for some of those we spoke to.

> People with a blue bib tried to give us information about political asylum. I wanted to seek asylum. I knew a little bit about it because of what had happened to my father. But I wasn't able to. The European police asked questions. There were interpreters. The first question was 'Would you like to work in Italy?' I said yes and they said okay, go. And I went...The next day they told me I had to leave and they gave me a piece of paper on which was written that I had to leave Italy in seven days. (Côte d'Ivorian man aged 20)

Others felt that people of particular nationalities were being favoured during the process of grouping and categorising people. There were also cases of irregularities with police officers accused of beating people, as well as sometimes turning a blind eye and allowing people to leave.

> The policeman had said I had driven the boat, he said it was me and then he beat me...I said I was Palestinian to get away from a policeman who had beaten me on the boat. (Egyptian man aged 29)

On arrival in reception centres many people expressed gratitude for being rescued. These feelings were particularly evident among those from West and Central African countries who had often left Libya without a clear destination in mind or people to connect with upon their arrival (see also Chapter Four). These views were also expressed by people who had only recently arrived and were unsure of the reception system, knew little about Italy and had not yet formed well-defined ideas about what to do next.

The situation for those arriving in Greece was very different (see Chapter 2) with chaotic scenes that unfolded on the Greek islands with literally hundreds of thousands of refugees and migrants arriving over the second half of 2015 to be met by an array of CSOs and volunteers (Box 7.3).

Box 7.3: The humanitarian response in Greece

At the outset of the unfolding humanitarian emergency there were only very few civil society support structures on the islands, indeed only on Lesvos and Samos. Examples included Lesvos Solidarity (known as Pikpa) in Mytilene and some local activists in northern Lesvos, and a lose Greek–Turkish network called Kayiki (boats). The findings from our research on Lesvos in the last three months of 2015 indicate that only two organisations – MSF and Pro Asyl (Germany) – anticipated what was to come and set up additional structures. From the summer of 2015 onwards, local volunteers were the only people assisting the newly arrived, sending reports and calls for support to alert and mobilise others (Hernandez, 2016). Within weeks, dozens of national and international CSOs, for example, Boat Refugee Foundation (NL), Drop in the Ocean (Norway), life guards from Spain and hundreds of volunteers rushed to the scene. Smaller CSOs and concerned individuals took responsibility for coordinating and organising the response. Some manned the lookouts and beaches to coordinate rescue and arrival; others organised medical screening facilities, dry clothes, food and water for those who arrived; others arranged transportation to transit camps managed by other agencies. Some were also active in the reception centres, either in the informal spaces prior to or after registration, while others covered the departure spaces, notably the port of Mytilene where many of our interviews were conducted.

The humanitarian response was also seen on mainland Greece, including in the port of Piraeus, in Athens and later in Idomeni on the border with Macedonia and indeed all along the Balkan route. This network was sustained by a second line of people arranging delivery of non-food items (clothes, tents, sleeping bags, medicines) and thousands of donors who were often mobilised through online campaigns and via social media. While some of the larger CSOs have been criticised for doing too little too late, these smaller agencies and their volunteers provided immediate support and assistance to hundreds of thousands of people arriving on the beaches of southern Europe, saving hundreds of lives. They emerged as a fifth force not only complementing state agencies, international organisations, international and national CSOs but indeed bearing the brunt of the emergency response. As a result, two of them – Lesvos Solidarity and the Hellenic Rescue Team – subsequently received the United Nations' Nansen refugee award in 2016.[6]

All of the 215 refugees and migrants we spoke to in Greece were met on the beach, or shortly after, by CSO staff or volunteers, who provided food, water, information and sometimes transportation off the beaches.

> We arrived on Lesvos island 16 days ago. Once we arrived, we took off our wet clothes and wore dry ones, and started walking. We walked for four or five hours to the camp. We were just following other people who were walking too. On our way to the camp some foreigners gave us food and water. (Afghan man aged 19)

Despite the efforts of humanitarian organisations and volunteers, the picture that emerges from our interviews with stakeholders as well as with refugees and migrants themselves is one of chaos and disorganisation. Many talked about the shocking reception conditions, especially in Moria camp. Experiences were of severe overcrowding, chaotic delivery of services, a lack of food, as well as violence from other refugees and migrants and the Greek police.

> There were 4,000–5,000 people in the camp. We were like animals in there. It was terrible. The police were yelling, swearing and shouting at us. It was filthy dirty. (Syrian man aged 47 travelling with his wife and three children aged 12, 9 and 6)

These accounts of the poor conditions and chaos on Lesvos are supported by multiple reports from journalists, volunteers and CSO staff which circulated widely throughout social media and the international media during that period, as well as our own observations while on the island. Consequently, camps were not referred to by those we spoke to as places of safety in which they could sleep and recover from the trauma they had left behind, or endured on their journey. Chaos and violence in the camps arose out of the need to find places to sleep and food to eat, but especially from the desire to be registered by UNHCR as quickly as possible. The camps on Lesvos were not – at that point – intended to be long-term reception centres, but rather short-term stopping places offering an immediate humanitarian response and to enable people to move off the island quickly. As UNHCR and other organisations struggled to deal with the number of people arriving, fights broke out in the queues for registration. Interviews with our respondents revealed clear confusion in terms of registration procedures, with some being fingerprinted and photographed and others not. This led to discontent and fighting.

> We spent six days in the camp, Moria. It was too crowded. Everybody was trying to get in the registration area; it was chaotic. People broke their arms and legs in the mud, rain. The police were beating people up, they were firing tear gas. (Hazara Afghan man aged 20)

As the situation deteriorated, the people we spoke to on Lesvos frequently reported violence from the police, including three allegations of police officers using teargas in the Moria camp ostensibly to calm residents. As refugees and migrants were reliant on the registration document in order to purchase a ferry ticket in the port, clashes also broke out there.[7] In addition to the clashes between the different nationalities, locals were also accused of attacking refugees and/or contributing to the violence.[8] In response to the clashes the Greek government sent riot police and troops.

Moria camp was terrible. I couldn't believe what I was seeing. My life in Syria was better than what I encountered in the camp. The police were beating people up. We waited in the queue. Our whole group managed to get in the container for registration, apart from me and my son. Something happened inside the container, and the police officer came out shouting. I was in the front. He hit me on the mouth with his shield. My mouth started bleeding. When he saw that I started bleeding, he left in order to beat up more people. After a while the police officers changed shifts. The new police officers were much better. (Afghan man aged 32 travelling with his sister and her husband)

Europe: moving on or staying put?

Although our research was undertaken with people who had recently arrived in Europe, we were interested to know whether they intended to stay in the countries in which they had arrived – Greece, Italy and Malta – or whether they intended to move on to other countries. The difference in responses between those travelling via the Eastern and Central Mediterranean routes was striking. Virtually none of those who were interviewed in Greece considered Greece to be a country in which they would stay. There were exceptions: for example, a young Syrian man told us that his father had been living in Greece for 16 years and that he regarded the country as his second home. But most respondents regarded Greece as a stopping point on their way to other parts of Europe. They were aware of the country's difficult economic circumstances and did not believe that it would offer them the opportunity to secure employment and rebuild their lives. For those with families who had been left behind, the ability to work and send money back in the form of remittances was an important factor driving the decision to move on.

I am not going to apply for asylum here. There is an economic crisis in Greece. There are no jobs. I have heard that it is tough here. (Afghan man aged 21)

As was noted in Chapter Three however, not all of those arriving in Greece wanted to reach the countries of northern Europe: 20 of those we interviewed in Italy and Malta had travelled to these countries from Greece. Of these, 12 had travelled along the Balkan route through FYROM, Serbia, Hungary and Austria, before entering Italy from the North, and four had crossed the Adriatic by boat directly from Greece, landing in Southern Apulia. Some had decided that they wanted to get to Italy or Malta before crossing the Mediterranean. In Sicily, for example, we met a group of young men who had set off together from Syria and who were attempting to reach family in Malta. In Malta we heard about refugees and migrants who had been picked up by the authorities on the catamaran (ferry) from Southern Italy, confirming this account. Elsewhere, we spoke to people from Pakistan and Bangladesh who had paid smugglers to take them from their home countries directly to Italy via the Eastern Mediterranean and through Greece. This was a more expensive route than the Central Mediterranean, but they considered that it was likely to be less dangerous:

> The trip cost almost €5,000 because it was well organised by smugglers. Another possibility was to reach Europe through Libya…With a sum of €2,300 he could have arrived in Italy but in much more dangerous and longer way. (Pakistani man aged 27 travelling with his uncle and two cousins)

Others had made the decision to travel to Italy when they arrived in Greece. This decision was influenced, to a large extent, by the difficult economic conditions but also by concerns about racism and violence, including at the hands of far-right organisations and vigilante groups. This contrasted with the very positive humanitarian response that people often experienced on arrival, especially in some, although not all, of the Greek islands.

> In Greece there was a bad atmosphere. Foreigners were treated badly also by public officials. In a public office, for example at the

post office or at the registry, officials called the police to report a foreign person instead of helping him. (Pakistani man aged 26).

The situation reported by those arriving in Italy was very different from that in Greece: two-thirds (67.5%) of respondents said that they wanted to stay. This was particularly clear among those who were originally from the Gambia, Nigeria and Ghana who had arrived through the Central Mediterranean route from Libya, and for Pakistani nationals, most of whom had travelled to Italy from Greece. The majority of those who wanted to stay in Italy had already applied for asylum by the time we met them.

The desire to remain in Italy was explained, in part, by the perception that it would be possible to find opportunities for employment particularly in larger towns such as Rome, Milan and Naples. Some indicated their intention to move away from smaller towns in search of opportunities for work once they had been granted permission to stay. Others expressed appreciation for the SAR operation that had effectively saved their lives and for the assistance that they had received at the hands of ordinary Italians and the local civil society who had welcomed them on arrival and helped them to settle. It was however also clear that, for many, Italy was the first country which they had reached where they felt safe. This reinforces our finding that the decision to cross the Mediterranean from Libya was a separate migration decision: people had originally intended to live and work in Libya but had been unable to do so due to escalating violence and insecurity. The accounts of these people speak more strongly to an experience of being forced to move than choosing to migrate for economic reasons.

As far as I am having my peace here, then I want to stay. (Gambian man aged 18)

We have nothing here, but at least we have life. (Nigerian man aged 20)

Circular migration and Dublin returns

While attention in 2015 was focused primarily on the dramatic, unfolding situation in the Mediterranean and on the beaches of Greece, for many the journey did not end there. Inadequacies in border controls and reception facilities provided opportunities for people to leave both Italy and Greece, enabling people to move onwards to other countries, usually where they could benefit from stronger support networks of friends and kin. Upon applying for asylum, however, they could be sent back. This is because the Dublin Regulation, which was described briefly in Chapter Two, requires an individual looking for protection in Europe to have their application processed in the first country in which they are identified. A European database of fingerprints and applications enables states to see where an individual arrived and determine whether they should be allowed to stay in the country where they have made the application or should be sent back to the first EU Member State in which they arrived. Although deficiencies in asylum and reception processes in Greece meant that, since 2011, there had been no returns to Greece under the Dublin Regulation, there continued to be enforced returns to other countries in Europe, including Italy. Under pressure from European institutions and Member States, the Italian government adopted a stricter approach to identifying people on arrival and recording fingerprints. For people who were unaware of the Dublin Regulation, being sent back to Italy came as a shock.

> I decided to go to Germany. I had some countrymen there and I knew that life for refugees was simpler. I re-applied for asylum but was sent back to Italy by the Dublin law in January 2016. For now, I still do not know the date of the commission. I'm stuck here, no papers, I can't even work (Sudanese man aged 36)

The experience of being returned was described as one of upheaval and disappointment sometimes with enforced separation from family members who had previously arrived in Europe (Box 7.4).

Box 7.4: From Jordan to Libya, Italy and Sweden then back to Italy: a Syrian family's story

Reem was 29 years old and living with her husband and three young children aged 3, 7 and 11 when we met her at a reception centre near Rome. The family was living in one room waiting for a decision about what would happen to them following their deportation from Sweden. Reem told us that the family had fled Syria in September 2013 with the help of a smuggler ('by the end of 2013 you could no longer pass freely') and had lived in Zaatari camp in Jordan for two months before moving to a house with financial assistance from her brother who has a shop in Saudi Arabia. She explained why they left Jordan: 'We wanted to live in Jordan, but the cost of living was increasing every day. Racism is spreading, too, and the Syrians were seen as a burden. We tried to ask for a visa to Saudi Arabia, to reach my brother, but it did not go well.'

The family took a plane to Tripoli where they lived until June 2015. Reem's husband worked in a small pharmacy owned by her brother but life was very insecure. The shop was subject to attacks and the children were not able to go to school. So the family sold up and used the proceeds to pay for the journey to Europe. After a difficult journey the family eventually arrived in Italy before travelling on to Sweden to join her cousins who were already living there. The family lived in Sweden 'in a beautiful house' for four months but at the end of the process they were returned to Italy under the Dublin Regulation. At the end of two years on the road the family distress was apparent:

> They say that for Dublin cases the road is very long and you have to wait. We wanted a quiet life. In Sweden we knew people. Our cousins live there. Here we are alone. We do not know anyone. We hope that God gives us the strength to start again.

Being sent back through the Dublin Regulation did not, however, necessarily represent 'the end of the road'. For some of those we interviewed it simply meant that they would need to start their journeys again.

I went to the north. I went all the way to Norway. I applied for asylum. They took fingerprints and then they asked me where I had arrived from. I said from Italy. So they sent me back in a plane...Now I realise that I am a fool. I am thinking of trying to go to another country and not say anything, just ask for asylum. I have a friend in Germany. Maybe I'll go there. In Italy there is nothing for refugees (Eritrean man aged 20)

These cases draw our attention to circular patterns of migration within Europe after the sea crossing has been left behind. They also provide a very clear illustration of the failings of Europe's policy response and the flawed assumptions on which it was based.

Notes

[1] See https://eulogos.blogactiv.eu/2015/09/29/is-the-dublin-regulation-really-dead/ for a more detailed discussion. Countries such as Hungary argued that the end of the Dublin Regulation meant that they were no longer required to accept refugees, www.sandiegouniontribune.com/hoy-san-diego/sdhoy-hungary-declares-dublin-system-dead-will-not-2015nov11-story.html

[2] Data on arrivals accessed from UNHCR and IOM Global Migration Data Analysis Centre. Data on deaths from IOM Missing Migrants project https://missingmigrants.iom.int/region/mediterranean

[3] See www.mediterraneanmissing.eu/

[4] See https://missingmigrants.iom.int/region/mediterranean

[5] See www.nytimes.com/interactive/2017/06/14/world/europe/migrant-rescue-efforts-deadly.html

[6] UNHCR (2016) Greek Volunteers share UNHCR Nansen Refugee Award, 6 September 2016, www.unhcr.org/uk/news/press/2016/9/57cdec884/greek-volunteers-share-unhcr-nansen-refugee-award.html

[7] See www.ekathimerini.com/201248/article/ekathimerini/news/greek-authorities-send-troops-police-to-lesvos-after-migrant-clashes

[8] See www.ibtimes.co.uk/migrant-crisis-troops-sent-lesbos-tensions-between-between-migrants-locals-turns-violent-1518677

EIGHT

Rethinking Europe's response

We conclude by examining the EU's response to increased migration in 2015 as well as policy developments in 2016 and early 2017. As noted in Chapter Two, the late, chaotic and uncoordinated nature of the response was not simply a consequence of the large numbers of people arriving. Migration across the Mediterranean, while larger in scale than anything seen previously, was small when compared with the scale of displacement elsewhere, most notably in countries neighbouring Syria (Turkey, Lebanon and Jordan), the population of the EU[1] and the relative wealth of the 28 EU Member States. The 'migration crisis' was simply the lens through which a number of other issues came to be viewed and arguably magnified.

Moreover, the findings of our research lead us to conclude that the EU and individual Member States *contributed* to the 'crisis' because their response was based on a series of flawed assumptions about the dynamics of migration across the Mediterranean. As the voices and experiences of the refugees and migrants presented in this book have shown, the nature of journeys, the routes taken and the factors that led people to get on a boat to Europe were far more complex than was typically presented. While the EU was successful, eventually, in reducing the number of arrivals through the Eastern Mediterranean route, it has done little to address the factors that led people to leave their homes in the first place or to move on from the places in which they initially settled. Addressing these factors will require a much more nuanced, longer-term approach.

The 'migration crisis' in context

So much attention has been paid to Europe's 'migration crisis' as a problem of numbers and scale that there has been a tendency to overlook the fact that this was just one facet of a trajectory of multiple crises (Kjaer and Olsen, 2016; Chryssogelos, 2016; Drozdiak, 2017) (Box 8.1). The crisis began not in 2015 but back in 2008 with a global financial crisis which triggered the European financial and debt crisis associated with far-reaching austerity policies. This had already affected the social order and undermined social coherence and trust in the European project which successively reinvigorated right-wing and populist political movements and parties. At the same time there was a wider, partly violent, reconfiguration of the post-cold war world order and the rise of new and mostly illiberal powers, most notably in Russia and Turkey, but also in Saudi Arabia and Iran.

During the 2011 Arab Spring, people across the Middle East and North Africa rebelled leading to a crisis of unjust governments in the wider neighbourhood of the EU. The uprising in Syria was followed by violent repression by the Assad government and a civil war. The Syrian governments' violent response, backed by Russia, followed by the rise of the IS, first in Iraq and later in Syria, led to a war during which entire cities were razed to the ground. There was a failure on the part of the international community to prevent this from happening, a failure of international politics and a crisis of war. This led to a humanitarian crisis in the affected cities and regions, including the siege of Aleppo and a subsequent crisis of displacement. Violent repression also followed the end of the Morsi government and a brief flowering of democracy in Egypt, while 2014 saw the break-down into factional conflict in Libya. Conflict in the EU's immediate neighbourhood was further reinforced by the advances of Boko Haram in Nigeria and a fresh war in South Sudan.

Box 8.1: Not one crisis but many...

In our discussions with stakeholders, and in our broader reading of politicaɪ ᵪ
policy documents, we encountered a range of views on the nature of the 'migration
crisis'. Our analysis leads us to conclude that it was symptomatic of, and became
shorthand for, a range of economic, political, foreign policy and humanitarian
crises taking place at the national, regional and global scales:

- a global financial crisis;
- a European financial and Euro-zone crisis, most notably the Greek debt
  crisis;
- an EU foreign policy crisis related to the rise of new and mostly illiberal
  powers (Russia, Turkey, Iran, Saudi Arabia);
- a political crisis in the Arab countries ('Arab Spring');
- a crisis of war and civil war, most notably in Syria, Iraq and Libya;
- a security crisis related to the rise of terrorism (especially IS, Boko
  Haram) and manifesting itself in Nigeria, Turkey, Brussels, Paris, London
  and different parts of Germany;
- a humanitarian crisis in war-torn countries and subsequent crisis of
  displacement;
- a humanitarian emergency in neighbouring countries (Turkey, Jordan,
  Lebanon);
- a personal crisis for refugee and migrants making the journey;
- a humanitarian crisis in the countries of first arrival, most notably Italy
  and especially Greece;
- a humanitarian crisis along the Balkan route;
- a crisis of the external border controls of the EU;
- a crisis of the sovereignty of EU;
- a moral crisis in relation to the search and rescue (SAR) effort;
- a crisis of identity for the EU and individual Member States manifested
  in public hostility towards refugees and migrants and the rise of the far
  right.

It was largely as a consequence of these events, combined with the
failure to provide protection and livelihood opportunities in the region,
that people were compelled to leave their homes, some of whom
continued their journeys crossing the Mediterranean and arriving in
Greece and Italy in 2015. Greece, which already had a dysfunctional

asylum and reception system and had been deeply affected by the economic crisis of 2011 and the severe austerity policy imposed by the EU, was overwhelmed by the increased number of arrivals leading to a crisis of refugee reception which was exacerbated by the EU's failure to manage the situation. This led to a humanitarian crisis on the Greek islands as well as along the Balkan route. In other words, what happened in 2015 became a 'migration crisis' not simply because so many people crossed the Mediterranean to Europe, but because of the inability of EU governments to deal with it (Balfour, 2016). The lack of control over borders and the building of new fences by some countries, most notably Hungary, to keep people out led, in turn, to a sense of crisis in the sovereignty of the EU which fuelled repressive policy responses and furthered the rise of illiberal political forces. This negatively affected the European integration project and finally resulted in a political crisis in, and of, the EU itself.

Too little, too late

What, then, was the EU response to increased migration and how did it contribute to this sense of 'crisis'?

The first point to make is that *the EU was slow to respond*, not only in terms of providing additional assistance to support the regions in which refugees and migrants were living but also in relation to the movement of increasing numbers of people travelling across the Aegean to Greece and then onwards across Europe. It was not until April 2015 that a ten-point action plan was presented by the EU Commission and a special meeting convened by the European Council (see Box 8.2). By this time thousands of men, women and children had already died crossing the Mediterranean Sea, including up to 1,200 people who drowned when two boats capsized that same month. These deaths were arguably the result of the end of Operation Mare Nostrum which began in October 2013 but ended in October 2014 due to concerns that SAR served as a 'pull factor'.[2] This, in itself, led to a focus on the Central Mediterranean route at precisely the time that numbers were starting to increase on the Eastern Mediterranean route. For instance, the EU NAVFOR operation launched in June 2015 targeted the waters between Libya and Italy but not the Aegean.

Box 8.2: Timeline of key EU policy events, October 2013 to February 2017

18 October 2013	Italy begins Operation Mare Nostrum.
19/20 December 2013	EU Council welcomes a 38-point plan by the Commission aimed at reducing journeys to the EU and reinforcing Frontex.
8 April 2014	EU Border Assistance Mission (EUBAM) in Libya discontinued due to security concerns.
26/27 June 2014	The European Council agrees key priorities for the next five years, which includes prioritising the Common European Asylum System and addressing root causes of irregular migration.
September 2014	Bulgaria begins the construction of a fence on the border with Turkey.
1 November 2014	Operation Mare Nostrum ends and is replaced by the Frontex-led Operation Triton.
20 April 2015	European Commission presents a ten-point plan of immediate action in response to the 'migration crisis'.
23 April 2015	Special Meeting of the European Council following the deaths of 1,200 people in the Mediterranean calls for the Valetta Summit and tripling of resources for Operations Triton (Italy) and Poseidon (Greece).
13 May 2015	The European Commission adopts a European Agenda on Migration.
27 May 2015	The European Commission puts forward the first package of proposals including the emergency relocation of 40,000 people.
22 June 2015	EU NAVFOR Med Operation, a naval operation against smugglers and traffickers in the Mediterranean, is launched.
25/26 June 2015	EU leaders agree to the relocation of 40,000 people from Italy and Greece, the resettlement of 20,000 more, the establishment of 'hotspots' in Italy and Greece, and other measures on return, readmission and cooperation with third countries.

24 August 2015	Germany's Federal Office for Migration and Refugees announces that it will not return Syrian refugees to Greece under the Dublin Regulation.
09 September 2015	European Commission puts forward a second package of proposals which includes an emergency relation proposal for 120,000 people, permanent relocation mechanisms for all Member States, a common list of safe countries of origin and a Trust Fund for Africa.
10 September 2015	Denmark suspends ferry lines and introduces borders controls with Germany.
14 September 2015	Germany introduces temporary border controls with Austria.
18 September 2015	The construction of a fence between Hungary and Serbia is completed.
22 September 2015	Relocation is agreed for an additional 120,000 people.
23 September 2015	State leaders pledge an extra €1 billion to international organisations and state agencies aiding refugees in the Middle East.
15/16 October 2015	The Joint Action Plan between EU and Turkey is announced.
18–21 October 2015	Slovenia restricts its intake to 2,500 arrivals a day.
25 October 2015	EU leaders agree to a 17-point plan of action during a meeting on the Western Balkans route.
12 November 2015	At the Valetta Summit the leaders of EU and African states agree an action plan focusing on five priority domains.
19 November 2015	FYROM government announces that only Syrians, Afghans and Iraqis will be allowed to cross the border from Greece.
29 November 2015	The EU–Turkey Joint Action Plan is agreed.
28 December 2015	Frontex initiates Operation Poseidon Rapid Intervention.
18–19 February 2016	The EU Council adopts a further conclusion on the migration crisis.
9 March 2016	FRYOM completely closes border with Greece.
18 March 2016	The EU–Turkey Agreement comes into force.

4 May 2016	The European Commission puts forward a series of proposals to reform the Common European Asylum System.
7 June 2016	The European Commission issues the 'Communication on establishing a new Partnership Framework with third countries under the European Agenda on Migration'.
6 October 2016	The European Border and Coast Guard Agency is launched.
3 February 2017	EU leaders adopt the Malta Declaration which focuses on curbing smuggling into the EU through increased cooperation with Libya.

Second, from a very early stage *there was a failure on the part of EU Member States to share responsibility for dealing with increased arrivals in a pragmatic and principled way.* This would not only have reduced the distress and anxiety experienced by those who arrived on the Greek beaches, but would also have taken the political 'heat' out of the situation, creating space for different kinds of policy responses. One policy tool that the EU had at its disposal, for example, was the Temporary Protection Directive,[3] which was created in July 2001 in response to mass displacement in the countries of the Former Yugoslavia. This could have provided a straightforward, pragmatic response to the arrival of people fleeing the conflict in Syria, who constituted more than half of those arriving during 2015. Instead, responsibility for addressing the needs of those arriving on the shores of Europe was left largely in the hands of Greece and Italy, two EU countries which have, historically, managed arrivals in very different ways (see Chapter Two). This resulted in chaotic scenes on Greek beaches and the onward movement of large numbers of people through the Balkans to the countries of Northern Europe but also, as we saw in Chapter Seven, to other EU Member States including Italy and Malta. This exacerbated the sense of 'crisis' not only in terms of the failure to provide an appropriate humanitarian response but also with regard to the evident failure of EU border controls.

Towards the end of 2015 the EU started to develop a system of partly closed reception centres, so-called 'hotspots', which were first proposed by the European Agenda on Migration,[4] bringing to an end the self-organised onward migration that featured so prominently during 2015. Located at key arrival points in Italy and Greece, the hotspots were designed to inject greater order into migration management by ensuring that all those arriving were identified, registered and properly processed (European Parliament, 2016). Although development of the hotspots was initially sluggish, the system was fully functional by March 2016. However, the human rights situation, facilities, and management of hotspots has been widely criticised, including by EU bodies. The European Court of Auditors (2017), for example, concluded at the end of 2016 that reception facilities in both countries were still not adequate.

The failure of EU Member States to step up to their responsibilities was also seen in the delivery of the EU's proposed solution to the issues facing Greece and Italy, namely the relocation of tens of thousands of refugees to other EU Member States. The EU agreed, in 2015, to relocate 160,000 refugees from Greece and Italy to other EU Member States under a two-year scheme that was later amended to relocate around 98,000 refugees. The pace of relocation during 2016 was slow, with just 5% of the total (8,162 people) relocated to other countries by the end of 2016.[5] The scale of cooperation between EU Member States, and in turn the pace of relocation, improved significantly in 2017, with almost the same number of people relocated in the first four months of 2017 as in the whole of 2016.[6] Nevertheless, some countries (UK, Ireland, Denmark, Hungary, Poland and Czech Republic) were either not part of the scheme at the outset or have failed to deliver on their pledges.

These two sets of policy failures – the failure to respond quickly and the failure to share responsibility – are symptomatic of a third, cross-cutting problem with the EU's response to increased arrivals across the Mediterranean, namely an emphasis on what Landau (2017) describes as 'the containment chronotype'. This means that *the focus has very much been on preventing or discouraging people from attempting to reach the EU territory* rather than providing protection and support or addressing the factors that caused people to move in the first place. Although the European Agenda on Migration adopted in May 2015 acknowledges the need for medium- and longer-term policies which would 'reduce the incentives for irregular migration', the emphasis has been on stopping people from crossing the Mediterranean by providing additional funding to Frontex, tackling smuggling networks, criminalising those involved in SAR and reception, and deporting individuals who are deemed not to have a right to remain (HRW, 2013; 2014; 2016a; Amnesty International, 2015; Jones, 2016).

The objective of 'keeping people out' rather than addressing their protection and other needs was reflected in the actions of EU Member States who, beginning with Hungary in September 2015, started to close their borders and build fences. In October 2015, the EU held a first High-Level Conference on the Western Balkans Route which focused on re-establishing border controls and sent a clear signal that the key objective was containment of the 'crisis' rather than protection and support for those on the move. From November 2015, FYROM, Serbia and Slovenia closed their borders to all but Syrians, Afghans and Iraqis, resulting in thousands of refugees and migrants being left stranded. In February 2016 FYROM became the last country to build a fence, this time to close off the border with Greece, sealing the fate of those in the country by preventing their onward movement through the Balkans. From March 2016, all borders beyond Greece were effectively closed to refugees and migrants crossing the Mediterranean by boat. The 'containment chronotype' (Landau, 2017) reached its logical conclusion in March 2016 when an agreement was signed between the EU and Turkey which traded enhanced border controls, readmission to Turkey and the resettlement of Syrians from Turkey to the EU in return for visa liberalisation and accelerated EU membership negotiations (Box 8.3).

Box 8.3: The EU–Turkey agreement[7]

On 18 March 2016, with fears of another 'summer of migration' in 2016, an agreement between the EU and Turkey came into force which aimed to stop the flow of refugees and migrants across the Aegean.[8] The key features of the agreement were as follows:

- from 20 March 2016 all new arrivals into Greece were to be returned to Turkey;
- for every Syrian being returned to Turkey from the Greek islands, another Syrian would be resettled from Turkey to the EU. Any further need for resettlement would be carried out through a similar voluntary arrangement up to a limit of an additional 54,000 people;
- Turkey was to take any necessary measures to prevent new sea or land routes for irregular migration to the EU;
- once irregular crossings between Turkey and the EU had ended, or at least had been substantially and sustainably reduced, a Voluntary Humanitarian Admission Scheme was to be activated;
- the fulfilment of the visa liberalisation roadmap would be accelerated with a view to lifting the visa requirements for Turkish citizens by the end of June 2016;
- the EU, in close cooperation with Turkey, would speed up the disbursement of the initially allocated €3 billion under the Facility for Refugees in Turkey;
- the EU and Turkey reconfirmed their commitment to re-energise the accession process.

The agreement rests on the flawed premise that Greece and the EU need not evaluate the individual protection needs of those arriving via the Aegean on the grounds that Turkey is a 'safe third country' or 'safe first country of asylum'. This is not, however, the case (Human Rights Watch, 2016c). As noted in Chapter Four, Turkey is a signatory to the Refugee Convention but maintains an important geographic limitation that excludes any non-Europeans from full refugee status. Syrians and other refugees can only benefit from a temporary protection regime. They continue to face many obstacles to registration, access to education, employment and healthcare. In the months following the deal, Greece's asylum appeals committees ruled in many instances that Turkey does not provide effective protection for refugees. As a result, all applications for asylum have to be assessed in Greece and there are now thousands of refugees and migrants living on the Greek islands in squalid and unsafe conditions (Amnesty International, 2016; 2017b).

Containment also features strongly in the EU's policy response to increased migration across the Central Mediterranean route. Although the focus in 2015 was very much on SAR, collaboration between the Italian and Libyan authorities intensified during 2016 and 2017. However as with Turkey, the aim of this collaboration has not been improving conditions for those living in Libya but rather preventing migration across the Mediterranean. The Libyan Coastguard has increasingly intercepted migrant boats at sea before they reach international waters and funds from the European Union, UK and the USA have been spent on housing migrants in Libyan detention centres in which conditions are known to be dire.[9]

Finally, the 'containment chronotype' has, over the last year in particular, shifted away from border closures towards the *growing use of development and other forms of assistance to leverage co-operation from countries and regions from which refugees and migrants have travelled*. The linking of development assistance with efforts to curb migration are not new: both the Rabat Process,[10] which began in 2006, and the Khartoum Process,[11] launched in 2014 are fora for European dialogue and cooperation with African countries which have increasingly linked the issue of development with the migration concerns of EU Member States. In both processes, the EU has placed an emphasis on border management, prevention of irregular migration, and improving regional protection. These efforts have intensified in the context of the 'migration crisis', most notably through the Valetta Summit and EU Trust Fund for Africa trend (Box 8.4). The securitisation of African borders conceptualises African migration as intrinsically directed towards Europe. The result is 'a repeated displacement of the border between EU and Africa vis-à-vis migratory flows every time more to the South, as well as the creation of a series of buffer zones in the African continent' (Gabrielli, 2016, 30).

Box 8.4: Valetta Summit and EU Trust Fund for Africa

The Valletta Summit on Migration, held in Malta in November 2015,[12] brought together European and African Heads of State and governments in an effort to reduce migration to Europe via the Central Mediterranean route. Leaders participating in the summit adopted a political declaration and an action plan designed to:

- address the root causes of irregular migration and forced displacement;
- enhance cooperation on legal migration and mobility;
- reinforce the protection of migrants and asylum seekers;
- prevent and fight irregular migration, migrant smuggling and trafficking in human beings;work more closely to improve cooperation on return, readmission and reintegration.[13]

The EU Trust Fund for Africa was created at the same time to address the root causes of instability, forced displacement and irregular migration and to contribute to 'good migration management.[14] The Fund is worth over €2.85 billion which includes over €2.64 billion from the European Development Fund and €202.4 million from EU Member States and other partners. The bulk of these resources are dedicated to the creation of jobs and economic development, especially for young people and women in local communities, with a focus on vocational training and the creation of micro and small enterprises. The other priority areas are supporting 'resilience' to support basic services for local populations, 'migration management', for example, to prevent irregular migration and fight 'human trafficking', as well as stability and governance, in particular by promoting conflict prevention, addressing human rights abuses and enforcing the rule of law. Eligible countries are: Sahel region and Lake Chad (Burkina Faso, Cameroon, Chad, the Gambia, Mali, Mauritania, Niger, Nigeria and Senegal); Horn of Africa (Djibouti, Eritrea, Ethiopia, Kenya, Somalia, South Sudan, Sudan, Tanzania and Uganda); North of Africa (Morocco, Algeria, Tunisia, Libya and Egypt).[15]

While additional funding for countries hosting the majority of refugees and migrants is welcome, there is growing concern about the use of development funding by the EU to further their own migration agenda on Africa. There is also concern that increasing cooperation with countries such as Sudan, whose leader President Al Bashir is currently wanted by the International Criminal Court for genocide in Darfur, will reduce rather than enhance the security of refugees and migrants living in these countries subsequently leading to more, rather than less, onward movement. Moreover because this approach is based on the assumption that migration in Africa is unidirectional and oriented towards the EU, it underestimates the importance of intra-African mobility and circular migration (Flahaux and De Haas, 2016). This could ultimately result in more, rather than less, permanent migration from countries of origin.

Flawed assumptions and expectations

The failure of the EU to respond effectively to the increased movement of people across the Mediterranean in 2015 was, in no small part, a problem of political differences and tensions within and between EU Member States (Crawley, 2016a; 2016b; Parkes, 2015). But it was also a consequence of assumptions and expectations which became deeply politicised over the course of 2015, employed by a series of different actors to justify, legitimate and reinforce policies which, while largely ineffective in addressing the issues that had led to the increased arrival of refugees and migrants, were intended to reassure the public that the situation was 'under control'. The evidence presented in this book points to four key assumptions that were, quite simply, wrong.

First, despite a huge body of academic and other evidence about the reasons for the increase in migration across the Mediterranean, the EU policy response was underpinned by *flawed assumptions about the reasons why people were on the move in the first place*, often through reference to an out-dated and widely critiqued 'push–pull' model (see Chapter One). This model underpins a raft of policy decisions, including the downscaled and then reinstated SAR operations which were, and still are, believed to make the prospect of migration more appealing (Hagen-Zanker and Mallett, 2016; McMahon and Sigona, forthcoming) (Box 8.5). Our detailed route-based analysis reveals the dynamic relations between drivers, opportunity structures and barriers to migration at various points along the journey and shows that the dynamics of migration to Europe were much more complex than this model assumes. It also shows significant differences between the experiences of those travelling to Europe via the Central and Eastern Mediterranean routes, as well as intra-route variations over time.

Box 8.5: Is search and rescue (SAR) a 'pull factor'?

While deaths in the Mediterranean are nothing new, it was the incident in October 2013 in which over 360 people died off the shore of the isle of Lampedusa (Italy) that marked the launch of one of the largest SAR operation in recent European history. Operation Mare Nostrum led by the Italian navy was launched on 23 October 2013 at a cost of €9 million a month. The mission operated on a two-pronged mandate, military and humanitarian, rescuing over 100,000 refugees and migrants in one year of operation.[16] Since that time SAR activities have arguably become one of the most controversial aspects of Europe's response to the 'migration crisis' (Steinhilper and Gruijters, 2017). There have been claims that SAR acts as a 'pull factor' for irregular migration, leading more people to attempt the crossing and, ultimately, more deaths. Partly as a result of opposition to SAR (most notably from the British government) and partly as a result of internal political dynamics in Italy, Mare Nostrum was replaced at the end of October 2014 by a Frontex-led operation with the involvement of several EU Member States.[17] The Frontex-led Operation Triton had a smaller budget, one third of Mare Nostrum, and a narrower mandate and operational scope. Whereas Mare Nostrum carried out proactive SAR across 27,000 square miles of sea, Triton's focus was on border surveillance and it operated only within 30 miles of the Italian coast.

Following a dramatic increase in casualties at sea in the early months of Operation Triton, especially two major incidents in April 2015 that caused the deaths of over 1,000 people, a decision was taken to expand Operation Triton's mandate and resources. Meanwhile since early 2014, with the launch of the Migrant Offshore Aid station (MOAS), privately-owned boats have played an increasing role in SAR under the general coordination of the Italian authorities. These operations have been subject to increasing media and political attacks including by EU's border agency Frontex, which has accused MSF and others of working in collusion with smugglers or at least helping them to carry out their deadly trade (Ponthieu, 2016). Others have strongly criticised this claim, arguing that it is the insufficiency of SAR capacity that causes the large number of deaths, and that migration is driven by factors unrelated to SAR.

This marks a new stage in an already existing trend, namely the criminalisation of non-state actors assisting and supporting migrants and refugees in Europe (Sigona,

2017). There is, however little or no evidence that SAR acts as a 'pull factor'. If SAR operations do encourage more arrivals and increased risks (for example, due to overcrowding or the use of lower quality boats), we would expect more arrivals and higher mortality risks in the high-SAR periods. An analysis of arrivals by Steinhilper and Gruijters (2017) found that the number of arrivals was highest in the low-SAR period, undermining the pull factor hypothesis. Rather than being caused by SAR, increased arrivals via the Central Mediterranean route are a reflection of political factors and the security situation in Libya together with the increased consolidation of smuggling activities (Pezzani, 2017). In the absence of a solution to the situation in Libya, it therefore seems reasonable to conclude that the end of SAR operations would lead to a significant increase in the already high, and growing, numbers of people who drown in the Mediterranean while seeking protection and a better life in Europe.

Second, the EU policy response was underpinned by *flawed assumptions about the nature of journeys to Europe*. The journey was assumed to be linear and quick with people leaving their countries of origin intending to travel to Europe, or specific countries within Europe. This meant that the 'in-between' was seriously neglected, a problem exacerbated by the focus on the countries to which people first moved as countries of 'transit' rather than countries in which it was possible for people to secure protection and rebuild their lives. The obsession with 'keeping people out' meant that the EU (and other countries) directed political and economic resources towards increased border controls at the expense of providing sufficient financial and other forms of support to those living in the countries hosting the majority of the world's refugees (Cosgrave et al, 2016).

Third, EU policy was, and continues to be, based on *flawed expectations regarding the impact of policy making on refugee and migrant decision making*. The extent to which policies which are intended to deter refugees and migrants can have the effect that is intended or assumed is challenged by the ad hoc and dynamic decision-making processes of the people on the move. Many of those travelling via the Central Mediterranean route did not originally intend to travel to Europe. Rather they went to Libya and other African countries primarily for work and only left when they felt unsafe. Others went to countries in the region and moved on when they did not feel safe (for example, Eritreans in Sudan), or when they could not find work or access education and healthcare for their children (for example, Syrians in Lebanon and Turkey) or if they had no sense of a future (for example, Afghans in Iran). Those who did specifically want to come to 'Europe' or particular countries within Europe often did so because of the general security and economic environment and/or presence of family and friends who could assist them.

Finally, as we saw in Chapter Five, the EU's response has been underpinned, and sometimes driven by, *flawed assumptions about the nature and role of smugglers and smuggling networks.* The objective of 'breaking the smuggling business model' ignores the fact that demand for smugglers will continue in the absence of opportunities to escape violence, conflict and unbearable poverty. It also assumes that most people smuggling is organised through large-scale criminal networks even though, as our research and that of others has shown, such activities are more often organised at a much more 'local' level and integrated into the wider economy. Without providing opportunities for refugees and migrants to travel legally and alternative livelihood opportunities for those whose income is dependent on the proceeds, people smuggling will continue to thrive.

Is the 'migration crisis' over?

From the point of view of Europe's political leaders, the 'migration crisis' has increasingly become a crisis of borders and thus of state sovereignty. After a humanitarian opening in 2013–14, refugees and migrants were, above all, perceived as a threat, and the priority was for the flow to be stopped. During late 2015 and early 2016, a number of European countries, most notably Austria, Germany and Sweden, 'recalibrated' their policy response to send a message to refugees and migrants, as well as the general public, that irregular migration would no longer be tolerated (Papademetriou, 2017). The EU claims that these policies have been largely effective and that the 'migration crisis' which dominated political and media debates in 2015 is now over.[18]

However, while the chaotic scenes which came to be associated with migration in 2015 have abated, at least in Greece, neither the conditions that fuelled it nor the demands for entry into Europe have changed (Papademetriou, 2017). The 'migration crisis' has not gone away: displacement continues on record levels but migration is simply confined to the regions, has become hidden or taken new forms.

First, *refugees and migrants are still crossing the Mediterranean to Europe*, albeit in smaller numbers than before. There were 176,906 arrivals in Greece compared to the 857,363 recorded in 2015, mostly arriving in the period up to March when border controls in the Balkans and in Turkey became effective. However, the number of people arriving in Italy increased by 16% in 2016. By June 2017, more than 70,000 people had arrived in Europe by sea (IOM, 2017) with increasingly large numbers of people being rescued in the Central Mediterranean and some emerging evidence of new routes developing.[19] And as we saw in Chapter Seven, the number and proportion of people dying as they attempt to enter Europe via the Central Mediterranean route, has significantly increased. In the meantime, more than 72,000 refugees and migrants continue to be stranded across Europe with limited opportunities for protection or integration. As of mid 2017, the majority were in Greece, where over 62,000 people were living in dire conditions (IOM, 2017).

Second, while there has been significant debate within the EU about the need to open up safe and legal routes, in practice *there have been few significant or meaningful developments in this regard*.[20] UNHCR projected there were 960,000 people globally in need of resettlement in 2016, including 316,000 in the Middle East and 279,000 in Africa.[21] In July 2015 the EU pledged to provide places for 22,504 persons in clear need of international protection. Not only was this pledge insufficient, it has not been delivered. As of 12 May 2017, 16,163 people had been resettled under the scheme, mainly from Turkey, Lebanon and Jordan (EC, 2017a). A further 5,695 Syrian refugees (of a potential 54,000) had been resettled from Turkey under the EU–Turkey agreement.[22] While the European Commission is committed, in principle, to significantly increasing the scale of resettlement through establishing a common EU Resettlement Framework,[23] the extent to which this policy objective can be delivered in the current political context is questionable.

Third, while the overall direction of EU policy in relation to smuggling has been through the lens of 'criminal activities' and 'smuggling business models' (Europol, 2016), *EU policies have most likely increased rather than decreased the demand for smugglers.* In April 2015, the EU Commissioner for Migration Dimitris Avramopoulos announced that Europe was 'at war' with smugglers and signalled the start of a new concerted effort on the part of the EU to 'break the smugglers business model'.[24] This was quickly followed by a renewed focus on tightening border controls through the use of FRONTEX patrols in the Mediterranean. Almost one year later EU Council President Tusk claimed that sending what he described as 'illegal refugees and migrants' back from Europe would similarly 'break the smugglers' business model'.[25] In practice both of these assertions have proved wrong. The evidence from our research suggests that smuggling is driven, rather than broken, by EU policy. Increased border controls may have reduced the number of people arriving by sea, on the Eastern Mediterranean route at least, but they have also resulted in an increase in clandestine efforts to reach Europe, in turn exposing vulnerable migrants to even greater physical and other risks (Cosgrave et al, 2016).

Finally, it is important to step away from the detail of the numbers which have captured the attention and political energies of the EU and look at the bigger picture. Not only has it been extremely costly in fiscal terms (ODI, 2016), *the EU's approach has also had a devastating effect on the lives of refugees and migrants both in Europe and globally.* In particular the containment strategy, reflected most explicitly in the agreement between the EU and Turkey but also in efforts to prevent migration from Libya, has undermined the moral authority of the EU, with 'ripple effects' for refugees living in others parts of the world and the international refugee regime more generally (Hargrave and Pantuliano, 2016). This will most likely serve only to destabilise already fragile political and economic situations, most likely leading to further outward migration, some of which will almost inevitably reach the shores of Europe. Ultimately Europe has no long-term strategy to deal with sudden mass influx from conflict when (not if) this occurs in the future. European leaders give the strong impression that they are hoping that Turkey, like a giant sponge, will continue to absorb future waves of refugees indefinitely. That is almost certainly wishful thinking. The 2016 attempted coup d'état in Turkey, and the ensuing crackdown, makes it less likely still.

The need for a new approach

As was noted in the introduction to this book, a new rights-based approach to migration in Europe is long overdue. This is increasingly recognised and is reflected in, for example, the creation of a UN Special Rapporteur on the Human Rights of Migrants (1999), Global Commission on International Migration (2003), Global Forum for Migration and Development (2007), European Union Agency for Fundamental Rights on the Human Rights of Migrants (2014), the EU's Global Approach to Migration and Mobility (2014) and Agenda on Migration (2015), the UN Sustainable Development goals (2015) which included migration for the first time, and more recently, the UN Global Summit for Refugees and Migrants (2016) leading to the Global Compact process.[26] Whether or not these institutions will deliver the promised results remains to be seen: in his 2015 report the UN's Special Rapporteur on the Human Rights of Migrants was rather critical but provided a long list of measures to be implemented and policy reforms needed (UN, 2015b). Much will depend on the political will of States and their willingness to take a longer-term view.

We conclude by drawing on the findings of our research to propose four key areas in which the EU needs to focus its policy efforts.

Addressing the drivers of migration

Perhaps more than any other area of policy making, it is far easier to say that the drivers of migration need to be addressed than to make it happen. Many of the conflicts from which the people we spoke had fled were deep rooted and long standing. But the fact that the drivers of migration are difficult to address does not mean that nothing can be done or that they should be ignored in the hope that they will simply go away.

Addressing the drivers of migration requires thinking through the consequences of a whole range of EU policies in the areas of human rights, humanitarian action, foreign affairs, international cooperation, development assistance, trade and investment (Castles et al, 2003). In the first place, the EU needs to acknowledge the drivers of forced migration, broadly defined, show leadership in finding political solutions to conflict as the key root cause of displacement, and step up its role in conflict prevention. Member States also need to think carefully about their role in creating and fuelling conflict and human rights abuse in some of the countries from which refugees flee including through the sale of arms and military equipment to countries which are involved in the repression of their own people or those in neighbouring countries. The EU needs to show greater commitment to promoting respect for international law including human rights law, international humanitarian law and refugee law. This means using its, not inconsiderable, political and economic power to leverage greater respect for human rights in the countries to which refugees and migrants first move.

Meanwhile as described above and in Chapter Two, the international community's response to the situation in the countries hosting the vast majority of the world's refugees has been wholly inadequate. There needs to be much more significant – and timely – assistance and investment in these countries to ensure that people do not feel the only alternative open to them are additional dangerous journeys over land and sea. This means providing refugees and migrants with rights to access the labour market as well as opportunities to educate themselves and their children.

Providing access to protection and rights

The international community as a whole has a role to play in addressing global migration challenges and refugee crises, including the crisis currently affecting the EU. However, the EU, its institutions, and its Member States have specific legal obligations to individuals on its territory and at its land and sea borders. EU governments are legally obliged to treat all of those who arrive in accordance with international law, including with regard to the right to seek asylum. This right is enshrined in the EU Charter of Fundamental Rights, and given practical effect in various EU laws and regulations. This obligation trumps other responsibilities including those related to the security of external borders. In this context the policy implications of our research are two-fold.

First, in the most immediate and practical terms, providing access to protection for refugees and migrants arriving in Europe through irregular channels means ensuring that humanitarian measures are easily accessible, robust and cover the widest geographic area possible, ensuring that reception facilities are adequate for the volume and diversity of arrivals, and ensuring swift and fair processing of asylum claims and appropriate action once status has been determined. It also means recognising that some conflicts are likely to have significant and long-lasting effects requiring the implementation of the Temporary Protection Directive and other emergency forms of assistance, including humanitarian visas, to avert the chaotic and desperate scenes with which the 'migration crisis' came to be associated.

Second, it means recognising that the need for protection cannot be determined by nationality alone. While 90% of those arriving in Greece in 2015 came from just three countries (Syria, Afghanistan and Iraq) in which there was well-documented conflict and human rights abuse there was also an implicit, and sometime explicit, assumption that having escaped the violence these people should remain in neighbouring countries, most notably Jordan, Lebanon and Turkey.[27] The decision to move to Greece and beyond was seen as being motivated primarily by economic factors. For Italy meanwhile, people came from a diverse range of countries and were perceived as being 'economic migrants' seeking employment and a better life even though most arrived from Libya where violence against black Africans in particular is well documented.[28] As a result, they were perceived as being 'less deserving' than those travelling through the Eastern Mediterranean route. This is reflected in the fact that refugee recognition rates decreased for those arriving in Italy over the course of 2015 (McMahon and Sigona, 2016).

Notwithstanding specific legal protections for refugees, the current use of simplistic categories of 'forced' and 'voluntary' migration creates a two-tiered system of protection and assistance in which the rights and needs of those not qualifying as 'refugees' under the legal definition are effectively disregarded (Metcalfe-Hough, 2016; Crawley and Skleparis, 2017). People's individual stories, their vulnerabilities and possible persecution cannot be understood without a proper assessment of their unique situation (MSF, 2016).

Creating safe and legal entry routes

Deterrence policies aiming at immobilising people in countries of origin or transit without concomitant access to protection, resettlement or humanitarian assistance will simply increase the extent of human suffering and may not, ultimately, reduce the scale of migration to Europe. The absence or slow realisation of safe and legal access to protection (resettlement or family reunification) increases the demand for illicit services, and thus also the exposure of migrants to smugglers and crime. It pushes people into taking ever more risky routes into and within the EU. At the same time, there is no credible evidence that SAR acts as a 'pull factor': few people are even aware that they might need to be rescued from the sea (almost invariably in the case of those boarding boats in Libya and Egypt). Ending SAR will simply increase the rate of death, as it has done in the past. The closure of borders, pushing refugees and migrants into taking even more difficult and dangerous routes, has the same effect.

An entirely different approach is needed instead, one that provides credible, safe, legal and accessible entry mechanisms for both those forced to flee and those who are looking for ways to support themselves and their families. The main policy implication of our findings is the need to open up safe and legal routes for protection. This includes significantly expanding current resettlement programmes, increasing humanitarian visas or establishing temporary international protection for those with a *prima facie* case for refugee status and increasing opportunities for family reunification. This would reduce the need for refugees and migrants to resort to dangerous irregular channels. The way to reduce the use of smugglers is not to close more borders or build more fences but to create alternative entry routes and address the drivers of irregular migration (OECD, 2015). This would include not only significantly more opportunities for refugee resettlement than currently exist but also a greater number of work visas (blue cards, seasonal workers) and visas for study (OECD, 2016; Toaldo, 2017). Some progress has been made with regard to family reunification: in 2015 there were around 47,000 approvals for family reunification of refugees and an additional 18,700 in Germany (EC, 2017b). However, most countries did not report the numbers and Germany largely suspended family reunification for refugees in 2016.[29] The provision of more safe and legal channels for refugees and migrants to reach the EU without having to risk their lives or resort to smugglers could reduce the scale of death in the Mediterranean. The development of such channels need not amount to an open-door policy: those arriving can be screened, have their protection needs assessed, and their entitlement to remain in the EU determined based on their international protection needs and any human rights imperatives. Those found, after a fair procedure, not to have such a basis to remain could be removed (HRW, 2015).

Moving beyond the politics of containment

We end this book as we began, by returning to the story of Michael and Niyat.

Michael and Niyat told us that they felt that they had no option but to leave Eritrea because of forced military conscription. During their time in the Sudan, Michael found work as an electrician and the couple were able to make a life for themselves. But the couple were constantly living in fear that they would be arrested and deported back to Eritrea, a fear made more likely as a result of the EU's policies of containment including the Khartoum Agreement which provides money to the Sudanese government in return for increased efforts to prevent onward irregular migration to Europe. Ironically it was this policy that potentially contributed to Michael and Niyat's decision to attempt the difficult and dangerous journey to Europe, engaging the services of smugglers to take them across the Sahara Desert to Libya and to board a boat with hundreds of other people that sailed off into the dark night.

Michael and Niyat were among the lucky ones. They were picked up by the Italian coastguard who saw that the heavily pregnant Niyat needed medical assistance and called the Maltese authorities to take her to Malta by helicopter, where the couple's daughter was born the following day. Many others are less fortunate.

For them, and for millions more who remain in countries and regions of origin, there is a real risk that efforts to stem the flow of migration to the EU will fail to address the conflict, violence and human rights abuses that drive both primary and secondary migration into Europe. In fact, EU policies may serve to exacerbate the situation even further.

The EU should design, implement, and monitor migration cooperation with third countries to ensure that the arrangements do not effectively trap people in abusive situations, prevent them from accessing fair asylum procedures, or lead to refoulement to places where they would be at risk of violence and persecution. It should also avoid cooperation with countries which are currently seeing significant outflows of displaced persons given the risk that such countries would manipulate the resulting processes to block their own nationals who fear persecution from seeking asylum in other countries. There is a chance, for example, that in the Khartoum Process the EU will channel significant funds through abusive governments in ways that end up harming people who try to flee persecution (HRW, 2015). The EU's humanitarian assistance should not be instrumentalised for political purposes or linked to strategic decisions aimed at preventing migration to the EU. If this is the case it will fail on both counts. Development is an important policy objective in its own right, not simply a mechanism for preventing migration to Europe. The people we spoke to, people like Michael and Niyat, mostly did not choose to come to Europe and if they could return to their homes and families they would. Directing the EU policy effort towards preventing or resolving conflict, challenging human rights abuse, and creating opportunities for employment in countries and regions of origin makes this much more likely to happen than simply trying to keep people out.

We risked our lives to come to Europe but now that we're here we realise it is just as hard as in other places…I just want to find a place where I can support my family and we can have a good life. I would love to go back to Eritrea because it is my homeland and that's where our family is, but this is not an option for us.

Notes

[1] While the arrival of 1 million refugees and migrants in 2015 was not insignificant, it added just 0.2% to the population of the EU which was 508 million at that time

[2] The UK government, for example, ended financial assistance for Mare Nostrum on the basis that 'search-and-rescue operations in the Mediterranean…[are] encouraging people to make dangerous crossings in the expectation of rescue. This has led to more deaths as traffickers have exploited the situation using boats that are unfit to make the crossing.' See www.theguardian.com/world/2014/oct/28/home-office-defends-uk-migrant-pull-factor

[3] Council Directive 2001/55/EC of 20 July 2001 on minimum standards for giving temporary protection in the event of a mass influx of displaced persons and on measures promoting a balance of efforts between Member States in receiving such persons and bearing the consequences thereof, http://eur-lex.europa.eu/legal-content/EN/TXT/PDF/?uri=CELEX:32001L0055&from=en

4   See https://ec.europa.eu/home-affairs/what-we-do/policies/european-agenda-migration_en

5   See https://ec.europa.eu/home-affairs/sites/homeaffairs/files/what-we-do/policies/european-agenda-migration/press-material/docs/state_of_play_-_relocation_en.pdf

6   See https://ec.europa.eu/home-affairs/sites/homeaffairs/files/what-we-do/policies/european-agenda-migration/press-material/docs/state_of_play_-_relocation_en.pdf

7   For a detailed legal analysis, see Peers (2016)

8   See www.consilium.europa.eu/en/press/press-releases/2016/03/18-eu-turkey-statement/

9   See www.theguardian.com/world/2017/jan/30/german-report-libya-abuses-pressure-migrant-flows

10 See IOM, 'Euro-African Dialogue on migration and development (Rabat Process)', www.iom.int/euro-african-dialogue-migration-and-development-rabat-process

11 See IOM, 'EU-Horn of Africa migration route initiative (Khartoum Process)', www.iom.int/eu-horn-africa-migration-route-initiative-khartoum-process

12 More at www.africa-eu-partnership.org/en/newsroom/all-news/2015-valletta-summit-migration

13 Available at www.consilium.europa.eu/en/press/press-releases/2016/03/18-eu-turkey-statement/

14 Available at http://ec.europa.eu/europeaid/eu-emergency-trust-fund-africa-factsheet_en

15 European Commission Press Release, 'EU Trust Fund adopts 90 million USD programme on protection of migrants and improved migration management in Libya', http://europa.eu/rapid/press-release_IP-17-951_en.htm

16 See www.theguardian.com/world/2014/oct/31/italy-sea-mission-thousands-risk

17 See https://ec.europa.eu/home-affairs/sites/homeaffairs/files/what-we-do/policies/european-agenda-migration/background-information/docs/frontex_triton_factsheet_en.pdf

18 See Traub, J. October (2016) 'Europe wishes to inform you that the refugee crisis is over', http://foreignpolicy.com/2016/10/18/europe-wishes-to-inform-you-that-the-refugee-crisis-is-over/

19 At the time of writing there were reports of growing numbers of refugees and migrants arriving on the beaches of Spain where the number of arrivals has been low. However, it was too soon to say whether this constituted a new 'route' as such. See, for example, www.telegraph.co.uk/news/2017/06/01/spain-bears-brunt-new-migrant-route/

[20] For example, in May 2015 the European Commission presented a comprehensive European Agenda on Migration which recognised the need to avoid those fleeing conflict and in need of protection having to resort to smugglers. See http://ec.europa.eu/dgs/home-affairs/what-we-do/policies/european-agenda-migration/proposal-implementation-

[21] See www.unhcr.org/558019729.pdf

[22] The EU–Turkey Statement of 18 March 2016 provides that for every Syrian being returned from Turkey from the Greek islands, another Syrian will be resettled from Turkey to the EU. Priority is given to refugees who have not previously entered or tried to enter the EU irregularly.

[23] See http://europa.eu/rapid/press-release_IP-16-2434_en.htm

[24] See www.independent.com.mt/articles/2015-04-23/local-news/Europe-is-already-at-war-against-smugglers-Commissioner-for-Migration-Dimitris-Avramopoulos-6736134333

[25] See www.ibtimes.co.uk/refugee-crisis-donald-tusk-urges-breaking-smugglers-business-model-1547619

[26] On 19 September 2016 the UN General Assembly unanimously adopted the New York Declaration for Refugees and Migrants directed at improving the way in which the international community responds to large movements of refugees and migrants, as well as to protracted refugee situations. The UN Higher Commissioner for Refugees has also been requested to propose a 'global compact on refugees' in his annual report to the General Assembly in 2018, to be considered by the Assembly at its 73rd session. More at http://refugeesmigrants.un.org/refugees-compact

[27] At the UN Summit for Refugees and Migrants, for example, EU Commissioner Avramopolous said that 'we need to make their journey to a safe place shorter and easier...those seeking protection should find a safe place as close as possible to their country of origin – even in a safe part of their country'. See http://europa.eu/rapid/press-release_SPEECH-16-3121_en.htm

[28] See for example, Reuters Italia (2015) 'Migranti, Alfano: rimpatriare quelli economici, Ue partecipi economicamente a 'hotspot'', http://it.reuters.com/article/topNews/idITKBN0OX1NI20150617

[29] See BAMF, 2017, https://ec.europa.eu/home-affairs/sites/homeaffairs/files/11b_germany_family_reunification_de_final.pdf

References

Achilli, L. and Sanchez, G. (2017) 'What does it mean to disrupt the business models of people smugglers?', *European University Institute Robert Schuman Centre for Advanced Studies Policy Brief*, Issue 2017/09, April

Amnesty International (2015) *Europe's Sinking Shame: The Failure to Save Refugees and Migrants at Sea*, London: Amnesty International, www.amnesty.org/en/documents/eur03/1434/2015/en/

Amnesty International (2016) *Trapped in Greece: An Avoidable Refuge Crisis*, London: Amnesty International, www.amnesty.org/en/documents/eur25/3778/2016/en/

Amnesty International (2017a) *International Report 2016/17: The State of the World's Human Rights*, London: AI, www.amnesty.org/en/latest/research/2017/02/amnesty-international-annual-report-201617/

Amnesty International (2017b) *A Blueprint for Despair: Human Rights Impact of the EU–Turkey Deal*, London: Amnesty International, www.amnesty.org/en/documents/eur25/5664/2017/en/

Angeli, D., Dimitriadi, A. and Triandafyllidou, A. (2014) 'Assessing the cost-effectiveness of irregular migration control policies in Greece', *MIDAS (Migration and Detention Assessment) Report*, www.eliamep.gr/wp-content/uploads/2014/11/MIDAS-REPORT.pdf

Balfour, R. (2016) 'Why are Europe's crises "existential"?', 4 March, Washington: German Marshall Fund, www.gmfus.org/blog/2016/03/04/why-are-europes-crises-existential

Barutciski, M. (1994) 'EU States and the refugee crisis in the former Yugoslavia', *Refuge* 14(3): 32–5

Belloni, M. (2016) '"My uncle cannot say 'no' if I reach Libya": Unpacking the social dynamics of border-crossing among Eritreans heading to Europe', *Human Geography* 9(2): 47–56

Betts, A. (2013) *Survival Migration: Failed Governance and the Crisis of Displacement*, Ithaca, NY: Cornell University Press

Bloch, A., Sigona, N. and Zetter, R. (2011) 'Migration routes and strategies of young undocumented migrants in England: a qualitative perspective', *Ethnic and Racial Studies* 8: 1286–1302

Campbell, J. (2017) 'Fleeing for freedom, Eritrean refugees are being abandoned by Europe', *The Conversation*, 14 March, http:// theconversation.com/fleeing-for-freedom-eritrean-refugees-are-being-abandoned-by-europe-73712

Carling, J. (2017) 'Refugees are also migrants. All migrants matter', Oxford: Border Criminologies, www.law.ox.ac.uk/research-subject-groups/centre-criminology/centreborder-criminologies/blog/2015/09/refugees-are-also

Castles, S., Loughna, S. and Crawley, H. (2003) *States of Conflict: The Causes of Forced Migration to the EU*, London: IPPR (Institute for Public Policy Research)

Chryssogelos, A. (2016) *The EU's Crisis of Governance and European Foreign Policy*, London: Chatham House

COE (Council of Europe) (2016) *Report of the Fact-Finding Mission to Turkey by Ambassador Tomáš Boček, Special Representative of the Secretary General on Migration and Refugees, 30 May–4 June 2016,* https://search.coe.int/cm/Pages/result_details. aspx?ObjectId=0900001680699e93

Collyer, M. (2010) 'Stranded migrants and the fragmented journey', *Journal of Refugee Studies* 23(3): 273–93

Collyer, M., Düvell, F. and de Haas, H. (2012) 'Critical approaches to transit migration', *Population, Space and Place* 18(4): 407–14

Cosgrave, J., Hargrave, H., Foresti, M. and Massa, I. (2016) *Europe's Refugees and Migrants: Hidden Flows, Tightened Borders and Spiralling Costs*, Overseas Development Institute (ODI) Report, www.odi. org/sites/odi.org.uk/files/resource-documents/10887.pdf

Crawley, H. (2016a) 'Crisis or opportunity? How European countries use refugees for political gain', *The Conversation*, www.medmig. info/crisis-or-opportunity-how-european-countries-use-refugees-for-political-gain/

Crawley, H. (2016b) 'Managing the unmanageable? Understanding Europe's response to the migration "crisis"', *Human Geography* 9(2): 12–23, https://www.sussex.ac.uk/webteam/gateway/file. php?name=hg-252-crawley.pdf&site=2

Crawley, H. and Skleparis, D. (2017) 'Refugees, migrants, neither, both: Categorical fetishism and the politics of bounding in Europe's "migration crisis"', *Journal of Ethnic and Migration Studies*, www. tandfonline.com/doi/abs/10.1080/1369183X.2017.1348224

Crawley, H., Düvell, F., Jones, K. and Skleparis, D. (2016a) 'Understanding the dynamics of migration to Greece and the EU: Drivers, decisions and destinations', *MEDMIG Research Brief* 2, Coventry: Coventry University, http://www.medmig.info/ research-brief-02-understanding-the-dynamics-of-migration-to-greece-and-the-eu/

Crawley, H., Düvell, F., Jones, K., McMahon, S. and Sigona, N. (2016b) *Destination Europe? Understanding the Dynamics and Drivers of Mediterranean Migration in 2015*, MEDMIG Final Report, Coventry: Coventry University, http://www.medmig.info/research-brief-destination-europe/

Crepeau, F. (2003) 'The fight against migrant smuggling: Migration containment over refugee protection', in J. Van Selm., K. Kamanga., J. Morrison., A. Nadig., S.Spoljar-Vrzina and L. Van Willigen (eds) *The Refugee Convention at Fifty: A View from Forced Migration Studies*, Lanham, MD: Lexington Books

De Haas, H. (2008) 'Irregular migration from West Africa to the Maghreb and the European Union: An overview of recent trends', *Migration Research Series*, 32, Geneva: IOM (International Organization for Migration), www.unhcr.org/49e479ca0.pdf

DGMM (Directorate General for Migration Management) (2016a) *Migration Statistics,* Ankara: DGMM, www.goc.gov.tr/icerik/ migration-statistics_915_1024

DGMM (Directorate General for Migration Management) (2016b) *Temporary Protection*, Ankara: DGMM, www.goc.gov.tr/icerik6/ temporary-protection_915_1024_4748_icerik

Douglas, R.M. (2015) 'Europe's refugee crisis: The last time around it was much, much worse', *The Conversation*, https://theconversation. com/europes-refugee-crisis-the-last-time-round-it-was-much-much-worse-47621

Drozdiak, W. (2017) *Fractured Continent: Europe's Crises and the Fate of the West*, New York: W.W. Norton and Co

Düvell, F. (ed) (2006) *Illegal Immigration in Europe: Beyond Control?*, Basingstoke: Palgrave MacMillan

Düvell, F. (2014a) 'Turkey's transition to an immigration country: A paradigm shift', *Insight Turkey* 16(4): 87–104

Düvell, F. (2014b) 'Transit migrations in the European migration spaces: Politics, determinants and dynamics', in F. Düvell, M. Molodikova and M. Collyer (eds) *Transit Migration in Europe*, Amsterdam: Amsterdam University Press, pp. 209–36

Düvell, F. (forthcoming) 'The "great migration" of summer 2015: Analysing the assemblage of key drivers in Turkey', *Journal of Ethnic and Migration Studies*

EASO (European Asylum Support Office) (2016a) *The Push and Pull Factors of Asylum-Related Migration: A Literature Review*, Brussels: European Asylum Support Office, www.easo.europa.eu/sites/ default/files/publications/The%20Push%20and%20Pull%20 Factors%20of%20Asylum%20-%20Related%20Migration.pdf

EASO (European Asylum Support Office) (2016b) *Annual Report on the Situation of Asylum in the European Union*, Brussels: European Asylum Support Office, www.easo.europa.eu/sites/default/files/public/EN_%20Annual%20Report%202015_1.pdf

EC (European Commission) (2015) *A European Agenda on Migration*, Communication from the Commission to the European Parliament, the Council, the European Economic and Social Committee and the Committee of the Regions, COM(2015) 240 final, http://eur-lex.europa.eu/legalcontent/EN/TXT/?qid=1432815601453&uri=CELEX:52015DC0240

EC (European Commission) (2017a) *Twelfth Report on Relocation and Resettlement*, Strasbourg 16 May 2017 COM(2017) 260 final, https://ec.europa.eu/home-affairs/sites/homeaffairs/files/what-we-do/policies/european-agenda-migration/20170516_twelfth_report_on_relocation_and_resettlement_en.pdf

EC (European Commission) (2017b) *Family Reunification of Third-Country Nationals in the EU Plus Norway: National Policies*, www.bamf.de/SharedDocs/Anlagen/EN/Publikationen/EMN/SyntheseberichteInform/ZuStudien/emn-wp73-synthese-familiennachzug.pdf?__blob=publicationFile

ECA (European Court of Auditors) (2017) *EU Response to the Refugee Crisis: The 'Hotspot' Approach*, Special report 25 April 2017, www.eca.europa.eu/Lists/ECADocuments/SR17_6/SR_MIGRATION_HOTSPOTS_EN.pdf

European Parliament (2016) *On the Frontline: The Hotspot Approach to Managing Migration*, Brussels: Directorate General for Internal Policies, www.europarl.europa.eu/RegData/etudes/STUD/2016/556942/IPOL_STU%282016%29556942_EN.pdf

Europol (2016) *Migrant Smuggling in the EU*, European Migrant Smuggling Centre, www.europol.europa.eu/publications-documents/migrant-smuggling-in-eu

Faigle, P., Polke-Majewski, K. and Venohr, S. (2016) 'Refugees: It wasn't really Merkel', *Zeit Online*, www.zeit.de/politik/ausland/2016-10/angela-merkel-influence-refugees-open-borders-balkan-route

Flahaux, M. and De Haas, H. (2016) 'African migration: Trends, patterns and drivers', *Comparative Migration Studies* 4(1) https://comparativemigrationstudies.springeropen.com/articles/10.1186/s40878-015-0015-6

Frenzen, N. (2011) '20th anniversary of the arrival at Bari, Italy of 15,000 Albanian boat people', *Migrants at Sea*, https://migrantsatsea.org/2011/07/29/20th-anniversary-of-the-arrival-at-bari-italy-of-15000-albanian-boat-people/

Gabrielli, L. (2016) 'Multilevel inter-regional governance of mobility between Africa and Europe: Towards a deeper and broader externalisation', *GRITIM-UPF Working Paper Series* 1, www.upf.edu/documents/3329791/0/L.+Gabrielli+-+GRITIM+WP+30+2016.pdf/4a034bb9-882d-9721-2cd6-20b133d63945

Gallagher, A.T. and David, F. (2014) *The International Law of Migrant Smuggling*, Cambridge: Cambridge University Press

Gillespie, M., Ampofo, L., Cheesman, M., Faith, B., Iliadou, E., Issa, A., Osseiran, S. and Skleparis, D. (2016) *Mapping Refugee Media Journeys: Smartphones and Social Media Networks*, The Open University/France Median Monde, www.open.ac.uk/ccig/sites/www.open.ac.uk.ccig/files/Mapping%20Refugee%20Media%20Journeys%2016%20May%20FIN%20MG_0.pdf

Gobat, J. and Kostial, K. (2016) 'Syria's conflict economy', *IMF Working Paper* WP/16/123, www.imf.org/external/pubs/ft/wp/2016/wp16123.pdf

Hagen-Zanker, J. and Mallett, R. (2016) *Journeys to Europe: The Role of Policy in Migrant Decision-Making*, ODI Insights, www.odi.org/sites/odi.org.uk/files/odi-assets/publications-opinion-files/10297.pdf

Hargrave, K. and Pantuliano, S. with Idris, H. (2016) *Closing Borders: The Ripple Effects of Australian and European Refugee Policy: Case Studies from Indonesia, Kenya and Jordan*, London: Humanitarian Policy Group, Overseas Development Institute, www.odi.org/sites/odi.org.uk/files/resource-documents/10862.pdf

Hernandez, J. (2016) 'Refugee flows to Lesvos: Evolution of a humanitarian response', *Migration Information Source*, 29 January, www.migrationpolicy.org/article/refugee-flows-lesvos-evolution-humanitarian-response

Hernandez-Leon, R. (2008) *Metropolitan Migrants: The Migration of Urban Mexicans to the United States*, Berkeley, CA: University of California Press

Horwood, C. and Hooper, K. (2016) *Protection on the Move: Eritrean Refugee Flows Through the Greater Horn of Africa*, Washington, DC: Migration Policy Institute, www.migrationpolicy.org/research/protection-move-eritrean-refugee-flows-through-greater-horn-africa

HRW (Human Rights Watch) (2013) *Unwelcome Guests: Iran's Violation of Afghan Refugee and Migrant Rights*, New York: HRW, www.hrw.org/report/2013/11/20/unwelcome-guests/irans-violation-afghan-refugee-and-migrant-rights

HRW (2014) *'I Wanted to Lie Down and Die": Trafficking and Torture of Eritreans in Sudan and Egypt*, New York: HRW, www.hrw.org/report/2014/02/11/i-wanted-lie-down-and-die/trafficking-and-torture-eritreans-sudan-and-egypt

HRW (2015) *The Mediterranean Migration Crisis: Why People Flee, What Europe Should Do*, New York: HRW, www.hrw.org/report/2015/06/19/mediterranean-migration-crisis/why-people-flee-what-eu-should-do

HRW (2016a) 'Yemen: Events of 2015', New York: HRW, www.hrw.org/world-report/2016/country-chapters/yemen

HRW (2016b) 'Iran sending thousands of Afghans to fight in Syria' www.hrw.org/news/2016/01/29/iran-sending-thousands-afghans-fight-syria

HRW (2016c) 'Q&A: Why the EU-Turkey deal is no blueprint', www.hrw.org/news/2016/11/14/qa-why-eu-turkey-migration-deal-no-blueprint

HRW (2017) *World Report 2017*, New York: HRW, www.hrw.org/world-report/2017

Humphris, R. and Sigona, N. (2016) 'Children and unsafe migration in Europe: Data and policy, understanding the evidence base', IOM (International Organization for Migration) Global Migration Data Analysis Centre (GMDAC) *Data Briefing Series* 5, http://publications.iom.int/system/files/gmdac_data_briefing_series_issue5.pdf

Ianchovichina, E. and Ivanic, M. (2014) 'Economic effects of the Syrian war and the spread of Islamic State on the Levant', *World Bank Policy Research Working Paper* 7135, http://documents.worldbank.org/curated/en/129431468044383360/pdf/WPS7135.pdf

İçduygu, A. (2015) *Syrian Refugees in Turkey: The Long Road Ahead*, Washington, DC: Migration Policy Institute, www.migrationpolicy.org/research/syrian-refugees-turkey-long-road-ahead

IGAD (Intergovernmental Authority on Development) and the Sahan Foundation (2016) *Human Trafficking and Smuggling on the Horn of Africa–Central Mediterranean Route,* Intergovernmental Authority on Development, http://igad.int/attachments/1284_ISSP%20Sahan%20HST%20Report%20%2018ii2016%20FINAL%20FINAL.pdf

IOM (International Organization for Migration) (2016a) *Mixed Migration: Flows in the Mediterranean and Beyond: Compilation of Available Data and Information 2015*, Geneva: IOM, www.iom.int/sites/default/files/situation_reports/file/Mixed-Flows-Mediterranean-and-Beyond-Compilation-Overview-2015.pdf

IOM (2016b) *Migration in Malta: Country Profile*, Geneva: IOM, https://integrafoundation.files.wordpress.com/2015/09/mp_malta_13july2016_0.pdf

IOM (2016c) *Study on Migrants' Profiles, Drivers of Migration and Migration Trends: A Research on the Socioeconomic Profile of Migrants Arriving in Italy*, www.italy.iom.int/sites/default/files/news-documents/Migrants%20Study%20-%20FINAL%20ENG%20VERSION%20-%20ELEC.pdf

IOM (2016d) *Migrant Smuggling Data and Research: A Global Review of the Emerging Evidence Base*, Geneva: IOM, https://publications.iom.int/system/files/smuggling_report.pdf

IOM (2017) *The Central Mediterranean: Migrant Fatalities*, Berlin: IOM Global Migration Data Analysis Centre (GMDAC), https:// gmdac.iom.int/the-central-mediterranean-route-migrant-fatalities-january-july-2017

Jansen, Y., Celikates, R. and de Bloois, J. (eds) (2014) *The Irregularization of Migration in Contemporary Europe: Detention, Deportation, Drowning*, London: Rowman & Littlefield International

Jones, R. (2016) *Violent Borders: Refugees and the Right to Move*, London: Verso Books

Kjaer, P.F. and Olsen, N. (eds) (2016) *Critical Theories of Crisis in Europe: From Weimar to the Euro*, London: Rowman & Littlefield

Koser, K. and Kuschminder, K. (2016) 'Understanding irregular migrants' decision making factors in transit', *Australian Government Department of Immigration and Border Protection Research Programme, Occastional Paper Series* 21 | 2016, Belconnen ACT: Department of Immigration and Border Protection, www.border.gov.au/ ReportsandPublications/Documents/research/occasional-paper-21.pdf

King, R. (2012) 'Theories and typologies of migration: An overview and a primer', *Willy Brandt Series of Working Papers in International Migration and Ethnic Relations* 3/12, Malmo: Malmo University, www.mah.se/upload/Forskningscentrum/MIM/WB/WB%20 3.12.pdf

Kyle, D. and Koslowski, R. (eds) (2011) *Global Human Smuggling: Comparative Perspectives* (2nd edn), Baltimore, MD: John Hopkins Press

Landau, L. (2017) 'The containment chronotrope: The European refugee "crisis" and shifting sovereignties in Sub-Saharan Africa', Paper prepared for *The Provocations of Contemporary Refugee Migration*, University of Florida, Gainesville 16–17 March, https://gallery. mailchimp.com/ebf39baff4da9ed51c02e6754/files/2880b840-773f-44f3-8089-c4357de85dba/LandauFloridaDraft.pdf

Long, K. (2013) 'When refugees stopped being migrants: Movement, labour and humanitarian protection', *Migration Studies* 1(1): 4–26

Lutterbeck, D. (2006) 'Policing migration in the Mediterranean', *Mediterranean Politics* 11(11): 59–82

Mainwaring, C. and Brigden, N. (2016) 'Beyond the border: Clandestine migration journeys', *Geopolitics* 21: 243–62

McMahon, S. (2012) 'North African migration and Europe's contextual Mediterranean border in light of the Lampedusa migrant crisis of 2011', *European University Institute Working Papers*, Florence: European University Institute

McMahon, S. (2017) 'The politics of immigration during an economic crisis: Analysing political debate on immigration in Southern Europe', *Journal of Ethnic and Migration Studies*, www.tandfonline. com/doi/abs/10.1080/1369183X.2017.1346042

McMahon, S. and Sigona, N. (2016) 'Boat migration across the Central Mediterranean: Drivers, experiences and responses', *MEDMIG Research Brief* 3, Coventry: Coventry University, www.medmig. info/wp-content/uploads/2017/02/research-brief-03-Boat-migration-across-the-Central-Mediterranean.pdf

McMahon, S. and Sigona, N. (forthcoming) 'Navigating the Central Mediterranean: Disentangling migration governance and migrant journeys', *Sociology*

Metcalfe-Hough, V. (2016) 'The migration crisis? Facts, challenges and possible solutions', *ODI Brief,* London: Overseas Development Institute, www.odi.org/publications/9993-migration-migrants-eu-europe-syria-refugees-borders-asylum

Micallef, M. (2017) *The Human Conveyor Belt: Trends in Human Trafficking and Smuggling in Post-Revolution Libya*, Geneva: The Global Initiative against Transnational Organized Crime

MPI (Migration Policy Institute) (2015) *Before the Boat: Understanding the Migrant Journey*, Washington, DC: Migration Policy Institute, www.migrationpolicy.org/research/boat-understanding-migrant-journey

MSF (Médecins Sans Frontières) (2016) *Obstacle Course to Europe: A Policy-Made Humanitarian Crisis at EU Borders*, Geneva: Médecins Sans Frontières, www.doctorswithoutborders.org/sites/usa/files/msf_obstacle_course_to_europe_report2.pdf

MSF (2017) *Dying to Reach Europe: Insight into the Desperate Journeys Eritreans Make to Reach Safety*, Médecins Sans Frontières, www.msf. org/sites/msf.org/files/msf-eritreareport.pdf

Neumayer, E. (2006) 'Bogus refugees? The determinants of asylum migration to Europe', *International Studies Quarterly* 49(3): 389–410

ODI (Overseas Development Institute) (2016) *Europe's Refugees and Migrants: Hidden Flows, Tightened Borders and Spiralling Costs*, www. odi.org/sites/odi.org.uk/files/resource-documents/10870.pdf

ODI (2017) 'Journeys on hold: How policy influences the migration decisions of Eritreans in Ethiopia', *Overseas Development Institute Working Paper* 506, www.odi.org/sites/odi.org.uk/files/resource-documents/11336.pdf

OECD (Organisation for Economic Co-operation and Development) (2015) 'Can we put an end to human smuggling?', *Migration Policy Debates* No. 9 (December). www.oecd.org/migration/Can%20 we%20put%20an%20end%20to%20human%20smuggling.pdf

OECD (2016) 'Are there alternative pathways for refugees?', *Migration Policy Debates* No. 12. (September), www.oecd.org/els/mig/migration-policy-debates-12.pdf

OHCHR (United Nations Human Rights Office of the High Commissioner) (2015) *Report of the Commission of Inquiry on Human Rights in Eritrea*, A/HRC/29/42, www.ohchr.org/EN/HRBodies/HRC/CoIEritrea/Pages/ReportCoIEritrea.aspx

Papademetriou, D. (2017) 'The migration crisis is over: Long live the migration crisis', Washington: Migration Policy Institute, www.migrationpolicy.org/news/migration-crisis-over-long-live-migration-crisis

Parkes, R. (2015) 'European Union and the geopolitics of migration', *Ulpaper* 1, Stockholm: Swedish Institute of International Affairs., www.ui.se/eng/upl/files/111585.pdf

Peers, S. (2016) 'The final EU/Turkey refugee deal: a legal assessment', *EU Law Analysis*, http://eulawanalysis.blogspot.it/2016/03/the-final-euturkey-refugee-deal-legal.html

Pezzani, L. (2017) *Blaming the Rescuers: Criminalising Solidarity, Reframing Deterrence*, London: University of London, https://blamingtherescuers.org/report/

Ponthieu, A. (2016) 'Bodies not bounties: smugglers profit from sea rescues but not clear alternative available, MSF Analysis http://msf-analysis.org/bounties-not-bodies-smugglers-profit-sea-rescues-though-no-clear-alternative-available/

Psimmenos, I. and Kassimati, K. (2006) 'Albanian and Polish undocumented workers' life-stories: Migration path, tactics and identities and Greece', in F. Düvell (ed) *Illegal Immigration in Europe: Beyond Control*, Basingstoke: PalgraveMacMillan, pp. 138–167

PRIO (2004) 'Afghan refugees in Iran: From refugee emergency to migration management', Oslo: International Peace Research Institute, www.files.ethz.ch/isn/38085/2004_06_16_CMI-PRIO-AfghanRefugeesInIran.pdf

Richmond, A.H. (1993) 'Reactive migration: Sociological perspectives on refugee movements', *Journal of Refugee Studies* 6(1): 7–24

Roch, M.P. (1995) 'Forced displacement in the Former Yugoslavia: A crime under international law?', *Penn State International Law Review* 14(1): 1–29, http://elibrary.law.psu.edu/cgi/viewcontent.cgi?article=1369&context=psilr

Ruttig, T. (2017) 'Afghan Exodus: Afghan Asylum Seekers in Europe (1) – The Changing Situation', *Afghan Analysts Network*, www.afghanistan-analysts.org/afghan-exodus-afghan-asylum-seekers-in-europe-1-the-changing-situation/

Salt, J. and Hogarth, J. (2000) *Migrant Trafficking and Human Smuggling in Europe: A Review of the Evidence*, Geneva: International Organisation for Migration

Sanchez, G. (2015) *Human Smuggling and Border Crossings*, London: Routledge.

Shelley, L. (2014) *Human Smuggling and Trafficking into Europe: A Comparative Perspective*, February, Washington, DC: Transatlantic Council on Migration, Migration Policy Institute

Skleparis, D. (2017) 'The Greek response to the migration challenge', *Working Paper* 5, 16 March, Athens: Konrad Adenauer Stiftung, www.kas.de/wf/doc/kas_48205-1522-1-30.pdf?170327142603

Sigona, N. (2017) 'NGOs under attack for saving too many lives in the Mediterranean', *The Conversation*, https://theconversation.com/ngos-under-attack-for-saving-too-many-lives-in-the-mediterranean-75086

Sigona, N. and Hughes, V. (2012) *No Way Out, No Way In: Migrant Children and Families in the UK*, COMPAS Research Report, Oxford: University of Oxford, www.compas.ox.ac.uk/media/PR-2012-Undocumented_Migrant_Children.pdf

Spijkerboer, T. (2016) 'Europe's refugee crisis: A perfect storm', *Border Criminologies* blog, Oxford: University of Oxford, www.law.ox.ac.uk/research-subject-groups/centre-criminology/centreborder-criminologies/blog/2016/02/europe's-refugee

Squire, V., Dimitriadi, D., Perkowski, N., Pisani, M., Stevens, D. and Vaughan-Williams, N. (2017) *Crossing the Mediterranean Sea by Boat: Mapping and Documenting Migratory Journeys and Experiences*, Final Project Report, Coventry: University of Warwick, www.warwick.ac.uk/crossingthemed

Steinhilper, E. and Gruijters, R. (2017) 'Border deaths in the Mediterranean: what we can learn from the latest data', *Border Criminologies* blog, Oxford: University of Oxford, www.law.ox.ac.uk/research-subject-groups/centre-criminology/centreborder-criminologies/blog/2017/03/border-deaths

Thorburn, J. (1996) 'Root cause approaches to forced migration: Part of a comprehensive strategy? A European perspective', *Journal of Refugee Studies* 9(2): 119–35

Tinti, P. and Reitano, T. (2016) *Migrant, Refugee, Smuggler, Saviour*, London: Hurst and Co

Toaldo, M. (2014) 'A European agenda to support Libya's transition', *European Council on Foreign Affairs Policy Brief*, www.ecfr.eu/page/-/ECFR102_LIBYA_BRIEF_AW_(2).pdf

Toaldo, M. (2015) *Intervening Better: Europe's Second Chance in Libya*, London: European Council on Foreign Relations

Toaldo, M. (2017) 'EU needs to offer work visas to bring migration under control', *Refugees Deeply*, 26 June, www.newsdeeply.com/refugees/community/2017/06/26/e-u-needs-to-offer-work-visas-to-bring-migration-under-control

Trauner, F. (2016) 'Asylum policy: the EU's "crises" and the looming policy regime failure', *Journal of European Integration* 38(3): 311–13

UN (United Nations) (2015a) 'Trends in international migration', *Population Facts* 2015/4, www.un.org/en/development/desa/population/migration/publications/populationfacts/docs/MigrationPopFacts20154.pdf

UN (2015b) *Report of the Special Rapporteur on the Human Rights of Migrants, François Crépeau*, A/HRC/29/36, www.ohchr.org/EN/HRBodies/HRC/RegularSessions/Session29/Documents/A_HRC_29_36_ENG.doc

UNHCR (United Nations High Commissioner for Refugees) (2011) 'Young Eritreans in Ethiopia face future in limbo', Geneva: UNHCR, www.unhcr.org/news/latest/2011/7/4e27de636/young-eritreans-ethiopia-face-future-limbo.html

UNHCR (2014) *UNHCR Observations on the Current Asylum System in Greece*, Geneva: UNHCR, www.refworld.org/docid/54cb3af34.html

UNHCR (2015) *The Sea Route to Europe: The Mediterranean Passage in the Age of Refugees*, Geneva: UNHCR, www.unhcr.org/5592bd059.pdf

UNHCR (2016) *Global Trends: Forced Displacement in 2015*, Geneva: UNHCR, www.unhcr.org/statistics/unhcrstats/576408cd7/unhcr-global-trends-2015.html

UNHCR (2017a) *Global Trends: Forced Displacement in 2016*, Geneva: UNHCR, www.unhcr.org/5943e8a34

UNHCR (2017b) *Mediterranean situation*, Geneva: UNHCR, http://data2.unhcr.org/en/situations/mediterranean?page=1&view=grid&Country%255B%255D=83

UNHCR and UNDP (United Nations Development Programme) (2017) 'Lack of funding putting help for Syrian refugees and hosts at risk, as Brussels Syria Conference set to open', Joint UNHCR/UNDP Press Release, www.unhcr.org/en-us/news/press/2017/4/58e340324/lack-funding-help-syrian-refugees-hosts-risk-brussels-syria-conference.html

UNHCR and World Bank (2015) *Forced Displacement and Mixed Migration in the Horn of Africa*, Eastern Africa. HOA Displacement Study Report No. ACS14361, Geneva and Washington, DC: UNHCR/World Bank, http://pubdocs.worldbank.org/en/892801436371029880/forced-displacement-horn-of-africa-Report.pdf

UNICEF (United Nations International Children's Emergency Fund) (2017) *Preparing for the Future of Children and Youth in Syria and the Region through Education: London One Year On*, Brussels Conference Education Report, http://wos-education.org/uploads/reports/170331_Brussels_paper.pdf

UNODC (United Nations Office on Drugs and Crime) (2011a) *Smuggling of Migrants: A Global Review and Annotated Bibliography of Recent Publications*, Vienna: UNODC

UNODC (2011b) *The Role of Organised Crime in the Smuggling of Migrants from West Africa to the European Union*, www.unodc.org/documents/human-trafficking/Migrant-Smuggling/Report_SOM_West_Africa_EU.pdf

Van Der Velde, M. and Van Naerssen, T. (eds) (2015) *Mobility and Migration Choices: Threshold to Crossing Borders*, London: Routledge

Van Liempt, I. (2007) *Navigating Borders: Inside Perspectives on the Process of Human Smuggling into the Netherlands*, Amsterdam: Amsterdam University Press

Van Liempt, I. (2016) 'A critical insight into Europe's criminalisation of human smuggling', *SIEPS Policy Paper*, Stockholm: Swedish Institute for European Policy Studies, www.sieps.se/en/publications/2016/a-critical-insight-into-europes-criminalisation-of-human-smuggling-20163epa/

Wissink, M, Düvell, F. and van Eerdewijk, A. (2013) 'Dynamic migration intentions and the impact of socio-institutional environments: The case of a transit migration hub in Turkey', *Journal for Ethnic and Migration Studies* 39(7): 1087–105

Zetter, R. (2007) 'More labels, fewer refugees: Remaking the refugee label in an era of globalisation', *Journal of Refugee* Studies 20(2): 172–92

INDEX

CPSIA information can be obtained
at www.ICGtesting.com
Printed in the USA
FFHW011122061218
49764786-54230FF